To my father

A talented and long ...
who taught me the r...

Acknowledgments

My thanks and my sympathy to all those editors who have put up with my negotiations and taught me those things that can be learned only by doing them. Over the years, one or another of them has been on the receiving end of every mistake an agent can make. And thanks to all my clients, past and present, who believed in me and have kept the wolf away from my door.

A number of editors, agents, and attorneys were kind enough to review one or more chapters, or to let me pick their brains in interviews or over the telephone: My thanks for valuable suggestions and comments to Arthur Abelman, Patty Breitman, Gay Bryant, Toni Burbank, Helen Freedman, Frances Goldin, Jerry Gross, Timothy Jensen, Karen Krieger, Edyte Kroll, Nick Lyons, Tom Quinn, and Al Zuckerman. And special thanks for very close and detailed readings by Brad Bunnin, Peter Beren, Bob Oskam, and Dodi Schultz.

My genuine respect and extra-special thanks to my editor, Carol Cartaino, who supported my efforts with lavish praise and enthusiasm, and who tempered my ego with a nineteen-page single-spaced critique, the advice from which has immeasurably improved this book.

Whatever stylistic felicities this book may have are due to the blue pencil wielded by by talented wife and ardent supporter, Felice Swados—lucky is the man with a companion as sweet as mine.

Contents

INTRODUCTION

Negotiating: neither as difficult nor as simple as you think

If you are the kind of person who pays the asking price for a used Old Crow bottle at a yard sale, or sends in a check for your entire phone bill even though you *know* you didn't make that call to Nome, or paid more than $5.00 for a "handmade" Italian wallet at an open market stall in Rome, you may not be the right person to negotiate your own magazine agreement or book publishing contract. You do have several options if you have an editor at a magazine or a publishing house who wants to sign up your book or article. The most obvious is to employ a literary agent.

Most agents—not all—are willing to negotiate for you if you present them with a *fait accompli,* an offer. However, you should not have a preliminary discussion about finances with an editor and then, feeling dissatisfied, turn to an agent. Writers have come to me in such circumstances (some even *after* signing a contract, which they then decided was unfair), and I have found it difficult, and sometimes impossible, to get for them the kind of "deal" I could otherwise have obtained for them. And if you are wondering, "What *is* my book or article worth?" the simple answer is: It is worth the maximum amount a publisher is willing to pay for it. We will discuss later how to arrive at an estimate of that. Lawyers too are negotiators, and there are a number who specialize in literary law—though they tend to be clustered in New York City and Los Angeles. They are as experienced and competent as any good literary agent, and they will negotiate for a fee instead of a percentage. In the long run, if your book is successful, this arrangement can save you a lot of money.

We will explore in the last chapter the whole issue of agents and lawyers. However, let us assume that you bought this book because you fully intend to do your own negotiating and want to see what it entails, what you can expect, what you have to know, what the small print in contracts means, what is the best possible "deal" you can make, and how to best go about getting it. Whether you have written a biography that Doubleday wants to sign or a craft book for Butterworth, or an article on digging wells that *Blair & Ketchum's Country Journal* is eager to publish or even a textbook or a young adult romance, this book should provide you with the tools and guidelines to understand what is involved in negotiating the contract.

In North America there are more than 16,000 trade book publishers (those that produce books sold to consumers through bookstores) and more than 65,000 (according to one creditable source) magazines. In 1984, more than 40,000 new books were published, as well as countless articles. Since there are only about 650 literary agents and no more than 250 literary lawyers, it is obvious that most writers negotiate their own contracts. (Even so, at the largest two dozen or so brand-name publishing houses, more than 80 percent of the books signed up are submitted by agents.) And don't think that all magazines or book publishers use written contracts; with many magazines and in the "small press" (independent or alternative press) world, which consists of more than 10,000 publishers, a handshake, a telephone conversation, or a confirming letter is as common as a written contract.

Negotiating your own book contract can be like buying a car: You can start the engine and listen, kick the tires, and say, "I'll take it. How much?" or you can follow the list of directions in *Consumer Reports* and make a thorough inspection of the car, check *Edmund's Used Car Prices*, and then do some hard haggling over the price. On the other hand, if you don't want to get the seat of your pants (or skirt) dirty looking under the car to see if there is an oil leak, or if the shocks are about to fall off, then the wise course would be to pay a reputable mechanic to inspect the car and tell you what condition it's in, and approximately what it is worth.

Correspondingly, if you feel that dickering over money—for that is often the primary issue in contract negotiations—where creative work is involved is somehow unclean or ill mannered, you owe it to yourself (or your heirs) to let an agent or a lawyer do it for you, rather than to accept the publisher's first offer and "standard contract" or "basic agreement." Most editors and publishers, whatever their reasons for being in publishing, are constrained by profit considerations whether they are owned by Gulf + Western or controlled by the founding family. And it follows that whether the product is a jar of pickles or the collected letters of Emily Dickinson, the operating maxim in dealing with the supplier (you, the writer) and the consumer (the book buyer) is: Buy cheap and sell dear. It seems only a question, then, of fair play—as opposed to, say, greed—for writers to use every possible resource available to secure for themselves a fair share of the profits from the sale of their products.

There are circumstances in publishing under which these precepts might not apply. Perhaps you have written a monograph for a university press (we will discuss such contracts too), and all concerned have only one motive: to disseminate esoteric information to a group of interested readers so few in number that both you and the publisher realize that the book will never earn back even the cost of producing it. Or you may be writing for a magazine funded by grants or patrons, or even by the publisher, that consistently fails to recover the cost of production. (There are certainly many of these.) Yet even here some negotiation is appropriate, though the goal is not to make money.

Under the new copyright laws passed in 1976 (a number of provisions are still pending), your work is protected from the moment of its conception—perhaps I should say its birth, because it has to be on paper, not just in your head—until fifty years after your death, even if it just sits in the bottom drawer of your desk. However, this protection is extended to you—when and if your article or book is published, or even mimeographed and offered for sale or distribution—*only if it is properly registered.* What if ten years after the publication in an obscure radical newsletter of your paper on capital punishment, it begins to make the rounds at various colleges, thanks to its word-of-mouth reputation, and the many copies that were photocopied and read? And what if a professor who is compiling a Freshman Composition reader wishes to include it in her book?

Some essays—take one of George Orwell's, for example—are virtually a *sine qua non* for all such readers. Each time an anthologist selects an Orwell essay, a fee of roughly $250 to $500 is paid by the editor of the anthology to the original publisher of the essay (or the current copyright holder). The latter turns over 50 percent (normally) of this fee to the author and will do so at least until the year 2000, when Orwell will have been dead fifty years. My point here is that whereas finances may not be a consideration *now*, they may be later—perhaps in ten or twenty years. Moreover, copyright protection is but one of a number of contractual issues that might sooner or later prove a headache for the cavalier writer.

In sum, it is just common sense to take the time and effort to understand the provisions of any publishing agreement and to try to negotiate it to your best advantage—or have someone competent do it for you. It may be the least interesting element of your writing career, or it may be the most awkward of moments for you in the long span of time between inspiration and publication, but it is nonetheless important.

It also pays to bring a sense of humor and a devil-may-care attitude with you into the negotiations. Many of the points you will attend to will probably never come to fruition, such as film, TV, radio, and stage rights (known collectively as "performance" rights); other provisions you may worry about may ultimately mean only a couple of dollars more or less for you or the publisher; some clauses you don't manage to change will mean that you will receive a certain sum of money within six months rather than in thirty days, and so forth. But even more significantly, less than one out of three books earns back the modest (or extravagant) advance against royalties that a writer generally receives, and the vast majority of books, even those that do earn back their advances, do not sell in great quantities, do not bring in much revenue for the author or the publisher, and do not require invoking most of the provisions you anguished over or fought for and lost.

Well, you might ask, if this is true, why make such a fuss about it? Why write an entire book about it? One obvious answer is that maybe your book *will* be one that surprises both you and the publisher and hits the best-seller list, or it may become a steady backlist title (such as *A Handbook of Electrical Wiring*) that goes into seven editions over a twenty-five-year period and earns a tidy income for its author. In other words—and this is true for agents as well as for writers—the time, effort, and anguish put into coping with contracts and negotiations involve a gamble, but an important one. It does for publishers too, who may put out upwards of one hundred books a year, gambling that at least thirty-three of them will pay for the cost of the other sixty-seven and even earn the house a small profit.

There are two more points to bear in mind. You are probably not as experienced or as cool about the outcome of the procedure as the editor is, so you should not expect to fare as well as Norman Mailer. Secondly, always remember that this *is* a "negotiation," a give-and-take situation. You will be frustrated and disappointed if you expect to be able to make all the contract changes suggested in this book. On the other hand, if you don't get everything you wanted in this contract, you are sure to do better the next time (provided your book is moderately successful!).

Finally, remember that there is no ideal contract, nor an ideal editor or publisher, for that matter; Alex Haley sued Doubleday for underprinting and inadequate distribution of his book *Roots,* even though it was a smash best seller. If you follow half the suggestions in this book and succeed in implementing *half of them* in a contract, you will do better than most writers who negotiate for themselves. Moreover, if your book is successful, the effort will pay off handsomely, and not just in dollars.

Note that publishing has its own language. It is almost impossible to avoid using the book industry's terminology and jargon in a discussion about contracts and negotiations. Nor, perhaps, is it advisable, since the writer who negotiates a contract will want to appear as experienced as possible and will be confronted by these terms during the process. Therefore, whenever I introduce such terminology or jargon for the first time in this book—such as "kill fee" or "mass market"—I provide a definition. One convention I frequently resort to is referring to "the publisher" as *he, they,* or *it,* depending on the context. Many decisions in publishing are consensual—that is, a number of executives are responsible for a single answer delivered by an editor. And it is also both common and convenient to refer to the publisher as an entity. In addition, a language problem arises in attempting to advise writers on how to negotiate a contract when there is no "standard" contract, and more than 65,000 magazines, 16,500 major book publishers, and 10,000 small presses and publishers of supplemental materials (depending on whose figures one chooses to cite.) This requires constantly resorting to qualifiers, parenthetical asides, and the tedious repetition of terms such as *conventionally, usually,* and *the rule of thumb,* for which practice I beg the reader's indulgence.

1

Magazine agreements

A *formal* agreement between a writer and a magazine, journal, or newspaper may consist of a printed contract or a letter of agreement (signed by both parties); an *informal* agreement may take the form of a letter from an editor, a scribbled memo or note, a phone conversation, or even just a canceled check. In the last case, endorsing a check generally signifies agreement to whatever terms appear on the back of the check, have been informally discussed, or are standard policy for that magazine (some attorneys will dispute this). Of the 65,000 or so magazines in North America, perhaps no more than half have a boilerplate (standard printed) agreement, though virtually all the major consumer magazines do.

Whether or not money is the primary issue in the agreement between a writer and a magazine, there are other important matters to consider, such as copyright, reprint rights, or the right to read and correct galleys prior to publication. Even those magazines that do have boilerplate agreements or issue some form of agreement letter do not generally spell out all the terms that should concern a writer.

Although the range of terms and fees is broad—from two free copies of the magazine to $3,000 or higher—a writer has less room for negotiation with magazines than with book publishers, whether the work is a short story, an article, or a poem. In part, this is due to the fact that a book can generate a certain amount of income for a publisher, the estimate of which may become the basis for negotiations. With magazines, there is rarely a correlation between a particular short story or article and the income for that particular issue. Naturally, *Esquire* might surmise that a short story by John Updike may increase that month's circulation by X number of copies, as would *Cosmopolitan* with an exclusive interview with Princess Diana, or *Playboy* with a piece by former President Nixon explaining his view of any political controversy. However, the number of writers capable of affecting circulation is but a handful compared with the thousands of us competing for the limited space in the magazine racks.

Professional writers (let us arbitrarily define them as writers who earn a meager but median wage of at least $6,000 or more a year from freelance writing) as well as celebrities—whether political, media, academic, or otherwise—do have considerable leverage in negotiating with the high-paying magazines. Those that pay handsomely, such as *Playboy, Esquire, Reader's Digest, The Atlantic,* and *Family Circle,* have a base rate of at least $2,500 to $3,000 plus expenses for an article 2,500 to 3,000 words long and generally pay one-half to two-thirds of that amount for short stories. For the extraspecial piece, such as any of those three mentioned in the preceding paragraph, they may pay—or bid for in an auction—as high as three to five times that amount. And there is a select handful of magazines, such as *The New Yorker* or *National Geographic,* that regularly pay $4,000 and upward for many of their articles.

Some professionals, and most celebrities, can virtually dictate the ideal nonfinancial terms for their pieces: no editing without the writer's approval, publication in a specific issue, and so forth. Even though it would be unrealistic to expect such an ideal arrangement, let's nonetheless use "a good deal" as a model in discussing finances and terms and explore at the same time the fallback positions and compromises that are more likely to be implemented in your agreement. But because the majority of magazines are more modest in their rates than those we mentioned, we will also examine their policies and conventions.

Whether or not you succeed in getting your requests accepted the first time around—no matter if it is your first story or your tenth article—it is important to begin acting like a professional, to understand what the stakes are, and to become more comfortable with the negotiation process. With each new publication not only will your confidence, exposure, income, and experience grow, but you will gain more respect and better treatment from editors and magazines, and your goal of becoming a professional will be a self-fulfilling prophecy: It is trite but true to say that if you *think* and *act* like one, you are more than halfway there.

Before we consider the details of magazine agreements it will be useful to identify several reference books that have gathered guidelines for both the rates and terms of several thousand magazines. Several are annuals, and it goes without saying that you should consult the most recent edition, even if the local library doesn't have it and some effort on your part is required to locate it. Policies and rates change rapidly for some magazines, and writers may immediately reduce the value and effectiveness of both their submissions and their negotiations by not being up to date. Just as important is being *au courant* on the staff, and here it is best to check the masthead of a current issue or call the magazine's offices. Sending a query or article to an editor no longer at that magazine may mean that your piece will be shunted off to the slush pile.

The major reference works are *Magazine Market Place* (annual), *Writer's Market* (annual), *Fiction Writer's Market* (annual), *International Directory of Little Magazines and Small Presses* (annual), *The Writer's Guide to Magazine Markets: Nonfiction*, and *The Writer's Guide to Magazine Markets: Fiction*. See the Recommended Reading list for an annotated description of their contents.

The writer who intends to submit a query or a finished piece or who is ready to negotiate terms with any magazine should first consult one or more of these reference books. Although it may be true that many of the magazines listed in them, particularly the more commercial ones, are apt to be a bit canny about disclosing their best rates and terms, the listing is still a starting point. Incidentally, circulation figures are not always a reliable measure of potential rates. One might think that a magazine with a circulation of 9.5 million, such as *Modern Maturity*, would pay a lot more than one with a circulation of less than half a million, such as *The Atlantic*; it doesn't. To a great extent, there appears to be little rhyme or reason to the rates magazines pay, save for the magazine's income in relationship to its expenses, and even this is not a totally reliable guide. Nor is advertising revenue; some magazines carry few or no ads, such as *Woman's World* (at least not for the first two years of publication, as of this writing), yet still pay relatively good rates.

Magazine negotiation is as likely to take place by mail as over the phone. In either case, the writer should already have prepared a list of priorities so that they can be discussed thoroughly but succinctly, bearing in mind that the magazine's guidelines—which the writer will already have gleaned from one or more of the foregoing reference works—are the starting point for the negotiation. These priorities may consist of the fee, the length, the territory, the rights granted, the delivery date, the share of the rights that the magazine retains, copyright ownership, expenses, the kill fee, the right to read and correct galleys, any restrictions on editing (especially for fiction and poetry), and so forth. Few magazine editors will raise more than half the points that ought to be spelled out, whether on the phone or in an agreement, so the writer must fill in the gaps. Furthermore, the priority list may be the basis for a letter of agreement that the magazine will send to the writer (though sometimes vice versa) for written confirmation—two copies, one for the magazine to keep, and one to be signed and returned to you—since many magazines are content with an oral agreement or a vague letter, though writers *never* should be.

Incidentally, some magazines issue a brief "letter of assignment" as their firm commitment but do not send a formal contract until a completed article is accepted. In this case you will nonetheless negotiate all the important points upon getting the assignment and make sure they are incorporated into the letter of assignment.

Finances. An editor will usually quote the magazine's fee for your piece in his or her initial discussion. This fee should, more or less, correspond to the rate you have gleaned from one of the reference works. It is therefore pointless to ask for $750 for a story from a magazine that lists $200 as its top rate, but—because many magazine rates are negotiable—it is not pointless to ask for $350, both because the listing from the reference book consulted is virtually out of date upon publication and because the magazine may not have been absolutely forthright about its top rates. At this juncture, a crucial bargaining chip may be just how much the magazine cares about getting your particular story or article—something you may have to sense. It is conventional for magazines to state their rates right off the bat, unlike book publishers, who may occasionally ask, "How much do you want?" I recommend *always* asking for 50 percent more than was offered, since in many instances this will result in a compromise offer. It doesn't hurt to bolster the argument by referring to a track record (if you have one), to the rates you have been paid elsewhere, or, in nonfiction, to the amount of research and effort that has gone or will go into finishing the piece (and this holds true when dealing with book publishing editors too).

In truth, I think that these arguments are basically irrelevant and easily countered by any editor. But their value is psychological: They put you on record as someone willing to press for a better deal, someone with experience and assertiveness, someone who will not simply accept all the terms that are dished out as standard for the writer who is happy just to see his or her work in print. Furthermore, even if the editor has no leeway to increase the rate (although in commercial magazines editors almost always do) the negotiation may elicit useful information, such as the fact that the fee is increased for the writer's second and third article or story (common for many magazines), or that the rate is determined by the length, the kind of piece, or its place in the magazine, or, in some cases, whether the piece appears in one or more regional editions, nationwide, or even in the international edition. In addition, the writer's initial assertiveness, whether effective in raising the fee or not, should make it easier to improve on the other terms of the agreement. The editor may now be more prepared to "negotiate" with the writer rather than to merely dictate the terms.

Of course, this assertiveness has to be handled diplomatically and in a low-key manner; moreover, this tactic is clearly more suitable for commercial magazines, as opposed to "little" magazines or literary journals. Also, a writer's natural leverage is greater with nonfiction than fiction; oddly enough, this is often the case with a query or outline rather than with a completed piece, since it is hard to imply or state that you need money for expenses to write the article when you have already finished it.

Assignment *vs.* Speculation.   Writers with good credits, or who write for a living, will almost never do a piece on speculation, unless, perhaps, the piece is a nontopical humorous or discursive essay. Or occasionally an established writer will write a piece "on spec" for a magazine because he or she may have failed to persuade the editor that the topic is as interesting or compelling as the writer believes it is—or for a number of other reasons—and will take the chance that if one magazine doesn't buy the piece, another will. (The piece done on spec is one that the magazine encourages a writer to complete—based on an outline or query—but withholds a firm commitment to pay for or publish until it is finished.) Since short stories are seldom offered to magazines on the basis of a query, this would not apply to fiction. Beginning nonfiction writers, or those who are stepping up in class, so to speak, or proposing a totally different kind of piece, may agree to write a piece on spec because they can offer no previously published materials that clearly indicate an ability to deliver the goods.

When a writer does accept this, it is nonetheless important to come to an agreement on virtually all other matters relating to publication, and not to wait until the piece is accepted. One should consider a commission on speculation as if it were a regular commissioned article. Moreover, there may be a slight possibility of getting the magazine to agree to a kill fee even if the piece is done on speculation. Editors and magazines—some of them—have hearts and are aware that as much time and effort will go into a commissioned work as into one done on speculation. Giving a kill fee for a piece written on spec is not standard policy at any magazine, but it can't hurt to ask.

Kill Fees. Most magazines that pay reasonable rates—say, $600 and upward—have a policy of paying a fee for a piece that is found unacceptable even after one or two rewrites or that, for one reason or another, is no longer suitable for that magazine when it is completed. This fee ranges from 10 to 50 percent but is commonly 20 to 25 percent of the agreed-on rate. When invoked, it also permits the writer to sell the piece elsewhere. Generally, the rate of the kill fee is more fixed than that for the article and is somewhat less negotiable. However, the writer who foresees unusual expenses in completing a piece will want to make sure either that the total cost of expenses is reimbursed in addition to the kill fee or that the latter is increased to compensate for the difference. This seems eminently fair and reasonable, though a writer may have to fight for it. Of course, kill fees and reimbursements for expenses should be incorporated into the agreement.

Payment Schedule. Again, writers with good credits or who write for a living will almost never agree to payment on publication but will insist on payment on acceptance. All magazines have an inventory, or "bank," a collection of finished pieces that can be drawn on to fill out an issue. Completed articles that arrive may be edited and immediately assigned to a specific forthcoming issue. Or they may be held up, depending on their timeliness, possible overlap with another piece, or the amount of space available in a forthcoming issue (which in turn is often determined by how much ad space has been sold for that issue). With no financial stake in a piece that doesn't have to be paid for until it is published, magazines can afford to be cavalier about their inventories. This is not to imply that all magazines that pay on publication are ruthless and greedy in filling their file cabinets without a second thought, but still. . . .

Those who write fiction and poetry are most often the victims of "payment on publication," and there is little redress for this, save to say, "No, thanks." Writers of articles that require considerable research or expense should be trebly resistant to payment on publication—or at least should make sure of being able to recoup expenses when the article is turned in. (Of course, a writer could accept this term and continue to submit the piece until it is sold to another magazine that paid on acceptance. At this point the writer could withdraw the piece from the first magazine by saying that he had changed his mind. Well, some of you cheat on your income tax, don't you? In either case, if you're caught at it, there are apt to be unpleasant repercussions.)

Here too, though, the writer with moxie could ask for half payment on acceptance and half on publication, regardless of the magazine's policy, by pleading poverty; some magazines do yield to this request.

Expenses. With nonfiction, many pieces require an outlay of expenses, which can range from those arising from half a dozen phone calls and $4.00 worth of photocopying to those from a round-trip ticket and two weeks of entertainment and room and board in Shanghai. There are three different levels of policy regarding expenses; they usually depend on the specific magazine. These levels are: limited expenses, reasonable expenses, and all incidentals. The first is the policy of most small-budget magazines, which may pay for long-distance calls, photocopying, and perhaps $.20 to $.25 per mile in case the writer has to do some driving around. "Reasonable expenses" will generally cover, in addition, any necessary but modest entertainment costs and airplane, train, bus, or taxi rides. "All incidentals" includes the previous two as well as the cost of any other special equipment required, secretarial or assistant fees (if necessary), an on-line computer search at a library, or even traffic tickets or medical fees for gunshot wounds if acquired in the line of duty.

Where significant expenses are required to complete an article, writers should have a tentative budget prepared in anticipation of a letter or phone call from the editor and will want to make this a priority issue in the negotiation. As well, the agreement should stipulate *which* expenses will be reimbursed, and it should be clear exactly when and how they are paid: upon receipt of appropriate invoices or receipts (these documents are always required) or upon the article's acceptance.

Length and Delivery. These two obvious issues should be settled during the initial negotiation. The writer may already have indicated in a query letter that the work will run to X number of words and can be completed in X number of months, but there is no reason to assume that, without a discussion, these matters are settled. Fees are often but not always related to length; therefore, should the editor ask for a piece longer than you propose, or request you extend it once it is turned in, you will want to ask for additional payment.

A deadline is equally important, and a casual oral agreement not only leaves the writer open for trouble but also doesn't provide that incentive that many of us need to sit down and do it. If you sense that the article will be late, even by as much as a week, immediately call and get an extension, because the editor may take your delivery date for granted and count on using your article in a specific forthcoming issue. And as with book publishers, late delivery can be sufficient cause for an editor to cancel the contract.

Artwork. Many magazines, especially the more commercial ones, will commission or secure the artwork (whether illustrations, photos, line drawings, or charts) if they think it suitable for a piece and may never even discuss the issue with the writer. On the other hand, an article may not seem to need art, whereas the writer may feel that it would enhance the work. This is a matter to raise *after* the magazine has agreed to do the piece, rather than at the query stage.

Magazines with modest budgets may expect or require that the writer supply photographs or illustrations, with or without additional compensation—hence the general wisdom that learning how to take your own pictures will help you sell your articles.

Some articles clearly require artwork, and this is a matter to raise during the negotiation. If you can supply professional-quality camera-ready artwork, then, once you have negotiated your fee for the article, by all means offer your work or that of a collaborator and suggest sending samples to the editor before a firm decision is made. (You don't want to do the artwork on spec, which is what you let yourself in for if the editor hasn't seen your work before giving the go-ahead.) Try to keep the negotiations for the article and artwork separate. Also, don't suggest the artwork of your cousin, friend, wife, or mother-in-law unless you have worked together professionally before. As a rule of thumb, all writers should keep personal and professional lives separate.

Rights. What rights is the writer assigning to the magazine? Well, what rights are there besides the obvious one-time publication? An article or short story might have film, radio, TV, and dramatic (performance rights) possibilities, in addition to several others. The most obvious is reprint rights; that is, the right to license another magazine or newspaper to reprint the same piece (known as second-serial rights). Then there are British and foreign rights, as well as the right to reprint the piece in a book, whether a collection from that magazine (e.g., *The Best of Esquire*) or an anthology (e.g., *Best Short Stories of 1985*). And there is always the increasing possibility, with the mushrooming growth of audio and video cassettes and computer software, of some further use or adaptation.

Fortunately, many magazines buy only "first North American serial rights," and the writer is spared the necessity of exploring this issue further. This is the right you want to raise first during the negotiation. Once this issue is broached, the editor will probably indicate whether the magazine's policy is to retain other rights, at which point the writer will ask for clarification. If the magazine insists on keeping other rights—a policy you want to resist or at least restrict—the writer will want to share in any revenue from an exercise of those rights for a minimum of 50 to 75 percent of the proceeds. But note that there are some magazines that insist on keeping all rights; this is a hotly contended issue among freelancers. Some editors will be vague about other rights only because "it hasn't come up before," or because the magazine has no fixed policy or even an informal one. The point is to limit the rights as much as possible and to get the editor to spell out exactly which ones he or she insists on retaining and for what share of revenue. Should the editor remain equivocal about rights, avoid burdening your negotiation with a prolonged discussion; simply add to your letter of agreement: "All rights not herein granted are reserved exclusively for the author."

The right most likely to be exercised, one that few writers explore on their own, is to have the same piece reprinted in another magazine or newspaper. *Reader's Digest*, the brass ring, may be the first possibility that comes to mind, but it is not the most probable. Assuming that most writers do not have the time or energy to search out second-serial publication, magazine by magazine—since most publications do not want already published pieces—the writer should query the syndicates. More than a handful of the one hundred or so national syndicators, listed in *Literary Market Place* and elsewhere, choose published materials selectively and try to give them a second life in newspapers and regional or national magazines (their listing will indicate whether they handle second-serial or not). For their efforts these syndicates take 50 percent of any revenue, which any writer should be happy to relinquish—all second-serial money is gravy.

Although the possibility for exercising any other rights is slim, there is no reason to let them remain with the magazine. When a magazine publishes a writer's work and retains first North American rights only, this right is generally "exclusive" in the territory given for the period of time during which the magazine is available for sale, whether it is a weekly, monthly, or quarterly publication. For most magazines, incidentally, the territory is generally North America, but some of the major magazines have international editions or the ability to license articles or stories internationally. Writers who don't have the time, energy, or resources to exploit foreign or reprint rights may wish to let the magazine do so, provided this magazine commonly makes the attempt, for an appropriate and negotiated share—at least 50 percent—of the revenue. In effect, the magazine acts as the writer's agent.

Copyright. Since the new copyright law went into effect in 1978, those writers whose works are published "collectively" in a magazine that copyrights the entire issue are assumed by law to own the copyright upon publication unless a formal transfer to the magazine is part of the writer's agreement. In effect, the writer grants certain rights to the magazine but retains the copyright (rights are "divisible" and can be sold or licensed separately, whereas copyright is indivisible). But to avoid any misunderstandings, a writer will nonetheless want to include on the first page of the manuscript the words "first N.A. rights" and to indicate in the letter of agreement that "copyright belongs to the writer," even though this is superfluous. Furthermore, if the writer sees from previous issues that the magazine or journal does not always carry a collective copyright (which sometimes happens with small literary magazines) he or she should register the copyright *before publication* simply by writing for (and then filling out and returning) form TX from the Copyright Office, Library of Congress, Washington, D.C. 20559. Even when the magazine has registered a collective copyright, it would be additional future protection to register the copyright anew in the writer's name, or at least to secure a letter of copyright assignment from the magazine after publication. The reason for this fuss is to be able to proceed against any future infringement without having to track down the previous publisher. Where the "little magazines" are concerned—which sometimes disappear after a year or two—this can be a lengthy, frustrating, and tiresome task. Why risk it?

Publication Date. Some magazines will indicate in which issue they intend to publish a piece if it is seasonal or topical, but in most instances they will be vague. Alas, most magazines cannot or will not guarantee publication in a specific issue—unless the writer has considerable leverage. Factors beyond the editor's control often determine how long a piece sits in the bank before it is published. It is not uncommon for an article to run a year or more after it is delivered, whether it was paid for on acceptance or not. I urge writers to try to negotiate a capping date for publication, after which time all rights revert to the writer, who still gets to keep the fee. This could be stated as: "Once we formally accept the article, we agree to publish it within one year; failing to do so, we agree to revert all rights to you without further procedure, and you will retain all monies paid."

A few magazines, if pressed, will agree to this, although many insist on an unreasonable date (perhaps within two years of accept-ance—one year or eighteen months should be the limit) and may al-so insist on sharing in the money from the second sale or being paid back in full. A writer should not have to forgo more than 50 percent of the proceeds from the second sale, no matter how high or low the fee. This is a touchy issue at many magazines, and most writers are disposed to leave it to the Fates. But surely it is fair—whether the writer is paid on acceptance or not—to expect to see your piece in print before your hair has turned completely gray, and it seems to me a matter worth fighting for. More likely, after six or more months have passed, the writer will call and find out that the piece is or is not scheduled and may extract at that time a promise that should the piece not be run by such and such a date, the magazine will revert all rights. (Get this in writing if you can.)

Editing.   Our last, and most tricky, issue concerns the magazine's discretion to edit (or to chop, rape, bowdlerize, and pulverize) a writer's work. I am still smarting from the publication of my own short but sweet (I thought) article in a recent issue of *McCall's*, which truncated my chatty 1000 words into a 125-word outline, devoid of whatever charms I presumed it had. The only notice I had was a brief note from the editor, who apologized for having to run the piece more than a year after it had been accepted (!) and for having to trim it "somewhat" (!). Anyone who writes for magazines over a pe-riod of years has this and other similar sad tales to relate.

Do you have any recourse at all? Poets and short-story writers should absolutely insist—in writing—that their work shall not be edited, revised, or cut without their approval. It is certainly fair and common for an editor to ask for some changes in fiction and even in poetry, although each writer has to decide how far he or she is will-ing to go. Furthermore, writers should ask to read and correct gal-leys. Some magazines will agree to this, provided that the turn-around time is quick. You can point out that errors or inaccuracies may have crept in (no editor wants that) and that you will give read-ing proof and turnaround time top priority. Because of production schedules at some magazines, you may have to settle for reading the "final edit," just before copy is sent to the typesetter.

With nonfiction, magazines are much more conventionally ar-bitrary and treat many pieces as newspapers do: cut 'em to fill the available space. One should ask for the right to (1) see or approve the edited/cut version and/or (2) correct galleys (at which time one can rant and rave and thereby perhaps be allowed to make some repairs if the piece has been unacceptably edited). The ability to have some control over the final version depends on the magazine's policy. Journals devoted to current events or the arts have much more respect for an author's work and will rarely edit, cut, or revise without consultation. The other factor depends on the writer: Just how important is the integrity of the piece to you? Those who write "lighter" nonfiction, such as my piece for *McCall's*, "How to Get More Help from Your Husband in Raising the Kids," are more apt to "take the money and run" (while simultaneously binding the wounds). Getting paid highly for fluff helps to soothe the ego. Those whose work requires more effort and research, or who feel that their professional life will be compromised by the publication of a badly cut work, will want to make editing a priority issue, if not a "deal breaker," in the negotiation. Given that many magazines do not have a formal agreement and will accept a writer's draft of one, what follows is a model letter that a writer might use as a contract. Remember to send two copies for signature, requesting the return of one.

With so many different boilerplate magazine agreements, there is little point to reprinting one here. Most issues covered in this letter are found in boilerplates or can be negotiated and inserted. Other matters that might be included in such a letter or an agreement are:

- inclusion of a tentative budget for travel expenses;

- fact-checking support by the magazine, or a sum agreed on to pay a freelance researcher for this chore;

- the writer's warranty and indemnification of the magazine for libel and accuracy (see p. 68);

- illustrations or artwork; how much, who provides it, and for what additional fee;

- what rights the writer shares with the magazine and for what split;

- whatever special provision may be called for by a particular piece.

The more articles a writer has published—assuming that some of them appear in national magazines—the more leverage that individual has in negotiating terms. Also, many magazines pay a higher fee for the writer's second or third article. However, unlike book publishers, many magazines are relatively inflexible and negotiating can sometimes mean to "take it or leave it."

January 8, 1986

Mary Editor
Good Health Publications
429 Elton Street
Boulder, Colorado 80080

Dear Ms. Editor:

I am delighted that Good Health wishes to commission my
proposed article, "Vegetarian Cooking for Pregnant Vegetarians."
I understand that the piece will run to approximately 2000 words,
and that you wish delivery of the completed article by April 1,
1986. Good Health agrees to buy first North American serial
rights and I will own copyright in the article.

Good Health agrees to pay $500 for the piece upon acceptance
and further agrees to provide guidelines for a rewrite if the
piece is unacceptable, and to permit me to read and correct
galleys, provided I return them within one week of receipt.
If Good Health decides that my revised version is unacceptable
and does not publish the article, it agrees to pay me a $100
kill fee within three weeks of said determination, at which
time all rights revert to me. Good Health may request up to
two rewrites.

It is further understood that Good Health will reimburse me
for routine expenses incurred in the writing of the article,
including long-distance phone calls, and that should extraordinary expenses be necessary, they will be discussed with
you before they are incurred.

If Good Health does not publish the article within twelve
months of acceptance, then all rights revert to me, and I
may keep the agreed-upon fee. All rights not herein granted
are reserved to me, and this letter, when signed by both of
us, will constitute our formal agreement.

Cordially,

Sally Author   For Good Health Publications

2

Trade book contracts

All trade book publishers have a basic printed contract known as the boilerplate. It varies in length from two to twenty or so pages and contains all the clauses and provisions necessary—from the publisher's point of view—to conclude a deal, except for some blanks here and there, such as for the author's name, the book's title, and the length and delivery date of the manuscript. When an editor says "our standard contract," he means the boilerplate with no changes, so that just the blanks are filled in; most contracts also have spaces for the amount of the advance, the royalty rates, the subsidiary rights split, and some other key considerations. A few contracts include the publisher's decisions on these terms as part of the boilerplate. Others have no specific dotted lines to be filled in for an advance or other key terms, but these are commonly inserted where there is blank space adjacent to that clause or can be inserted as "riders," which are any complete clauses added to a contract. "Provisions" refer to separate parts of any clause.

As is clear by now, there is no need to be daunted or intimidated by the printed word in contracts, for most authors and all agents make many changes on the boilerplate. Still, the problem for the initiate is not only which changes to make, but which changes *can be made*. That is, you want to know which clauses and provisions editors are willing to haggle over and which terms reflect fixed house policy or are so taken for granted by those in the industry that a writer's requests to change them will be met with great resistance or complete inflexibility. Also, what about riders you wish to insert? Are they common, unorthodox, or just plain way out of line?

Perhaps your primary reason for buying this book is to find the answers to those questions. In going over a sample contract clause by clause, we will examine the probable, possible, and unlikely, as well as suggestions for riders, additional provisions, and fallback positions. However, by no means should you expect to find *all* the contingencies or all the parameters discussed, if for no other reason than that every one of the 200 or so firms that I have dealt with has a different contract. In addition, many of them have different "house policies" regarding certain requests. Furthermore, some houses will occasionally abandon "fixed house policy" on one or more points if they want a book badly enough. Still, virtually all the pertinent issues will be explored in sufficient detail to cover 95 percent of the possible contingencies.

As we will see in more detail in the chapter on negotiating tactics, the solution to these uncertainties is partly a matter of common sense, learning the ground rules, and feeling your way through the negotiation with the editor (the truisms that apply to love and war and all other negotiations).

Any contract provides the opportunity for an almost unlimited number of changes, if for no other reason than that the possible contingencies are manifold. But of course a line must be drawn somewhere, and in drawing it we are guided by three factors: common sense, the amount of leverage the writer has, and the writer's priorities.

The leverage is dictated in large part by the writer's track record—if there is one—and by how much income or profit the house estimates the book can generate. Although it is very difficult for a writer to estimate these numbers—not to mention be "objective" about them—one can partly sense what they are in preliminary discussions with the editor concerning his or her sense of the market, the audience, the potential for subsidiary rights, and the initial strategy the editor has in mind for the book. Also, it is wise to ask the editor how many copies the house thinks it can sell the first year and how large is the projected size of the first printing. All these issues are guesstimated *before* an editor makes an offer. Clearly, then, the more optimistic the house's fantasy—though, in fact, these projections are normally conservative rather than extravagant—the more leverage the writer has both in the financial area and in the number of requests to make and have accepted. Tricky, isn't it? For this reason, agents often make multiple submissions or conduct auctions, for in these cases—provided more than one house wants the book—the amount of leverage is automatically extended to the limit of the house with the most optimistic fantasy. Moreover, in the heat of an auction, publishers frequently go beyond their initial estimates, on the assumption that if another house is willing to up the ante, the book may be worth more than they thought.

The writer should have a list of priorities prepared in advance of the negotiation (this list depends on what kind of book it is, the intended audience, and other factors germane to that particular book) and will have discussed and concluded the negotiations for some of them on the phone prior to receiving the contract. It may be, however, that upon receiving the boilerplate, the writer will discover some boilerplate clauses or inserted riders that are so unfair or unacceptable that they too now become priorities. For instance, it seems perfectly reasonable that the publisher of your first novel should have a right of first refusal on your second, and so you readily agreed to it on the phone. But when the contract arrives, the option clause contains a "matching option" provision. This means that if you don't wish to accept the publisher's offer for your second novel, you are free to submit it elsewhere, but when and if you do receive a better offer from another house, your original publisher has the right to "match" that offer and take the book. The problem is that many publishers do not wish to bid on a book, knowing that any offer they make may be matched and the book whisked away. So changing the option clause becomes a priority.

Once you have gone over the contract and noted all the changes you wish to make, list them in order of priority. If you have more than two dozen or so, you may be going over the line of common sense. On the other hand, it may be that the contract is so objectionable that you are beginning to think about going elsewhere. Bear in mind that in a negotiation you are going to do some compromising, probably in two areas: the actual terms or restrictions of a particular provision—say a 6 percent paperback royalty versus the 8 percent you wanted—and the total number of changes, deletions, or riders you wish to add. For instance, the editor may or may not agree to give you "approval" over a paperback reprint sale. It follows that by having a list of priorities, it will be easier for you to distinguish and fight for those that are most important, and to be more flexible about those that aren't.

It is also useful to bear in mind that by starting the negotiations with more requests than you expect to be approved and asking for higher amounts than you anticipate getting, you have room to compromise and fall back. Negotiators, whether editors or labor leaders, never start with their bottom lines, because both parties in a negotiation have to come away feeling that they won something. If you start with your bottom line, you can only lose. This is the way the game is played.

Before we go over the provisions of a sample contract, let me reiterate some points and set the stage and the context of the dialogue with the editor and for the negotiation itself. If you have followed my advice so far, you will have already prepared a list of no more than five to ten priority issues, although for some books you may have fewer. By letter, or more likely by phone, an editor will contact you and say, "We like your book and would like to publish it." She may then raise any reservations before making an offer: We need another sample chapter, would you be willing to cut the book, can you supply camera-ready artwork, can you deliver a completed manuscript by such and such a date, and so forth. Satisfied with your answers, the editor will then generally state an advance-against-royalty figure and may also suggest royalty rates, the territory wanted (which will almost always be world rights), the author/publisher share of subsidiary rights, and so forth (although a common first offer is just an advance and "our standard royalties").

Before discussing your priorities, you will want to express your delight and to ask the editor how she feels about the book, what she thinks about its possibilities, the size of the audience, what the tentative first printing may be, the list price, the first year's sales projection, and the subsidiary rights possibilities. You will *not* want to negotiate without this picture of the house's already prepared tentative expectations for your book.

At that point, if you are satisfied with the house's enthusiasm for the book, you may want to go over your list of priorities, although you might withhold further discussion of the advance until you have had time to calculate what a reasonable advance should be, based on the discussion of advances on p. 47. Incidentally, if I seem to stress the advance as the most important factor in your negotiation, this is my agent's bias. Some writers' lists of priorities may place the advance lower on the list.

Most likely, the editor will agree to some of your requests, reject some, and suggest compromises on others, although invariably she will have to consult with superiors about some of them. At that point, and *before* you have firmly agreed to *any* part of the offer, it is best to end the conversation by saying how thrilled you are, that you just want to let the good news sink in, and that you will talk again in a day or two. You need that time to consider the offer and to decide what you can live with and what you can't; that is, you may have to reshuffle your priorities.

In your second conversation you will negotiate and nail down the advance and the priorities—making it clear, however, that you will need to see and review the contract and work out the fine print before you are sure that you have a deal. Your third part of the negotiation should be in writing: that is, you will make a photocopy of the boilerplate, or the filled-in contract itself, which can take two to four weeks to arrive, send a letter summarizing what has already been agreed on, and write or type in the changes you want on the photocopy of the contract. Some of these will now constitute a second list of priorities.

Lastly, the editor will call you after receiving your letter and negotiate these remaining points. Sometimes this procedure requires half a dozen phone calls and several letters, sometimes just one call and one letter; it all depends. Don't hesitate to say, "I want to think that point over and will call you back." Any uncertainty should be recollected in tranquility. A reasonable number of changes to make in a contract ranges from about ten to twenty-five points; fewer means that you probably haven't gone over it carefully enough, more may mean that you are going overboard. What *is* important is to deal with all your contractual requests at the same time (and ditto for your first list of priorities); that is, do not bring up new requests on different occasions. As negotiating requires compromises and tits for tats, you are not playing by the rules if you conduct it piecemeal. For additional tips on negotiating, as well as a discussion of the process, see Chapter 4.

The following contract—from a well-known trade publisher—was chosen because it contained virtually all of the standard provisions and clauses found in trade contracts, was quite "fair" as a boilerplate, and was as free of legalisms, jargon, and ambiguities as any I have encountered. In using a negotiated contract, it will be easier to show not only which changes were made, but also the manner and language employed to do so. In some places I will also indicate other changes that might have been requested but weren't. The identifying label and the order of the clauses may differ from those in the contract the writer receives, and some separate clauses are merely embedded as provisions in clauses in other contracts, but the corresponding clauses and provisions are generally easy to identify.

Incidentally, as will be noted in this discussion, there are a number of instances in which I say, "This provision may not be found in other contracts." The reason is that this boilerplate has been recently revised by the publisher and is therefore more "up to date" than most, since publishers generally revise contracts, on an average, once every five to ten years. This contract is also therefore more explicit about many contractual issues, and more in line with current practices, than most.

AGREEMENT made this 28th of June , 19 85 , between
c/o The Balkin Agency
850 West 176th Street
New York, NY 10033
(hereinafter referred to as "the Author") and XXXXXXXXXXXXXXXXXXX
XXXXXXXXXXXXXXXXXXXXXXXXXXXXXXXXXXXXXXXXXXXXXXXXXXXXXXXXX
New York, New York XXXXX (hereinafter referred to as "the Publisher") with reference to a work tentatively entitled

XXXXXXXXXXXXX

(hereinafter referred to as "the Work").

WHEREBY, in consideration of the promises set forth in this Agreement, the Author and the Publisher agree that:

GRANT
1. The Author grants and assigns to the Publisher the sole and exclusive right to print, publish and distribute the Work in book form in the English language, in the United States of America, its territories, possessions and dependencies, Canada, the Philippines and through-out the world (hereinafter referred to as "the Territory") during the whole term of copyright and any renewals and extensions thereof, and the sole and exclusive right for such term to exercise or authorize the exercise of the other rights in and to the Work set forth in Paragraph 6 hereof in the Territory.

1. The Grant. This clause designates the territory that you are assigning "exclusively" to the publisher. Most contracts encompass three possible territories. The first covers world rights; that is, all countries in all languages. The second includes all English language rights; that is, the United States and its territories (the Virgin Islands, Guam, Samoa, etc.), possessions, and dependencies (the Philippines), Canada, and the British Commonwealth. In book publishing, the British Commonwealth is still more or less defined as the Victorian Empire and includes Wales, Scotland, Ireland, Australia, New Zealand, and a host of present and former protectorates, numbering as many as fifty countries, which range from Ascension to Zambia—although increasingly now some countries, such as Australia, are licensed separately. The third territory is the most restricted and consists of English language rights in the United States and its territories, possessions, and dependencies and Canada. Missing from this boilerplate clause is a provision found in most trade book contracts that states: "and nonexclusive English language rights throughout the open market, except for the British Commonwealth." This means that a publisher may sell the U.S. edition in any non-English-speaking country, such as Switzerland or Japan, but may have to compete there with any British edition published, *if* the writer has retained British Commonwealth rights, and *if* an edition is licensed and published in England.

Conventionally, the writer without an agent will assign world rights to the publisher, who will act as the writer's agent, so to speak, in attempting to license British and foreign-language rights and will share any revenue from these sales at a negotiable split (see clause #7). Agents generally retain these rights on their clients' behalf (but not always; it depends on the leverage), because they, in turn, have subagents in most major foreign countries, such as Italy, France, Germany, and, of course, England. Without a subagent, it is time consuming, difficult, and somewhat complicated to license these rights. It is definitely not recommended unless the writer has some reason to think that a particular foreign sale is a strong possibility. For example, a book on American-Japanese foreign relations or a novel set in Holland might be licensed in those respective countries.

If a writer with an appropriate book has the time and energy, there are two advantages to retaining British and foreign rights: The writer will retain 100 percent of any money from the license (but receive only 80 percent if represented by an agent and foreign co-agent), and—more importantly—the money from this license will not be deducted from the advance given by the U.S. publisher. If a publisher gives a writer a $7500 advance against royalties and controls foreign rights with a 75/25 split, then an advance from France of $2000 means that the author's share is $1500. However, in most cases, the publisher has the right to deduct this $1500 from the unearned advance of $7500, so that the writer now has an unearned advance of $6000. *If* the book sells in sufficient quantities to earn out the entire advance, then the writer eventually receives the 75 percent share of the foreign sale, generally at the time the second or third royalty statement is sent. But if the U.S. sales of books or rights don't bring in $7500 (about two out of three trade books do not earn out their advance), then the writer receives only the amount from royalties or the sale of rights that exceeds the original advance.

But this advantage must be weighed against the disadvantage of negotiating from a position of relative ignorance with a foreign publisher and the inability to monitor the publisher because of the distance. The solution to these problems is to get an offer and turn the matter over to a foreign agent (see *International Literary Market Place* for a listing of British and foreign agents).

In reality, no more than about one out of fifty books will "travel," so it is generally not worth the effort to retain 100 percent of foreign rights; or, let us say, it should not be a priority. In rare instances, it may be worthwhile to retain Canadian rights, if there is a strong reason to suspect that the book will particularly appeal to either English-speaking or French-speaking Canadians or if the author is a Canadian citizen. Of total North American books sales, roughly 5 percent is accounted for by Canada, and on these "export" sales, a publisher generally reduces the royalties by about half (books are generally "distributed" by Canadian publishers, rather than licensed). U.S. publishers strongly resist giving up Canada, so it isn't worth fighting for unless the writer thinks that a license and impressive sales are a probability. The reason for lowering the royalty rates is that the books are sold for export at a higher discount, and hence lower net receipts for the house.

The Grant clause assigns the specific rights granted to the publisher for the whole term of copyright (now fifty years after the author's death) and authorizes the publisher to exercise any of these rights—including subsidiary rights—on the author's behalf. As you will later note in the Termination clause, the publisher's rights to the book will end at some point if the book is no longer in print in any edition or is not under license to be reprinted by some other publisher, or it will end, under certain circumstances, thirty-five years after publication.

DELIVERY

2. (a) The Author shall deliver to the Publisher on or before December 20, 1985, two neatly typed, double-spaced copies of the complete manuscript for the Work approximately 90,000 words in length, acceptable to the Publisher in content and form.

2. Delivery. (a) The date agreed upon to deliver a completed manuscript. If a writer contracts a book on the basis of sample chapters, it is wise to agree to a date a least 25 percent later than one reasonably calculates is needed to complete the book. Most books are delivered late—we are all a bit too optimistic in our expectations—and although publishers commonly grant writers extensions, they can occasionally be sticky about it or even cancel the contract if they feel that the book is timely and likely to lose sales because of a later publication date, as might a book about a presidential election that appeared later than a year after the election. Some contracts emphasize the importance of the delivery date by including a phrase such as "since time is of the essence. . . ." This adds legal weight to any court case that might arise from this issue and diminishes a writer's potential legal argument based on what is common practice in the book publishing business (that is, accepting late delivery). Incidentally, the time to ask for an extension is not a week or a day before the book is due, but at the earliest moment a writer realizes that he or she will probably not make the deadline, even if this is six months before the stipulated date. The earlier it is requested, the more likely an extension is to be amicably granted, especially if the writer shows evidence of progress (sending some finished chapters with the request). Writers with generous delivery dates who request extensions shortly before due dates with little signs of progress are pushing their luck.

A key phrase worth discussing here is "acceptable to the publisher in content and form," which can be invoked if a book is contracted on the basis of an outline or an outline and sample chapters and the editor feels that the manuscript does not coincide with or live up to the implicit "promise" of the outline or sample. Conventionally (and as is spelled out here in provision [d]), the publisher has an implicit obligation to provide editorial assistance to help the writer revise the manuscript into one that *is* acceptable in form and content. This obligation has traditionally been open to interpretation up until the past few years, where several court cases, decided in the writer's favor (notably *Goldwater vs. Harcourt Brace Jovanovich*), have set a clearer precedent regarding the publisher's obligation. An author should expect, at the least, a letter detailing the substantive problems, with clear suggestions for rectifying them, and an opportunity to do so, if the editor finds the manuscript unacceptable.

> (b) On or before the delivery date set forth in subparagraph 2(a) hereof, the Author shall at Author's expense deliver valid written permission for use of any copyrighted material in the Work from the proprietor thereof (such permission to extend to all rights granted herein) and provide all drawings, maps, charts, photographs and all other illustrative material which Publisher deems necessary for the Work. If the Author fails to do so, the Publisher shall have the right to secure such permissions and/or to prepare or cause to be prepared any illustrative materials and charge the cost thereof to the Author.

(b) If a writer uses material from other copyrighted works, whether quotations, extracts, or entire chapters or sections, written permission from the copyright holder may be required, and it is the writer's responsibility to secure it. The publishing doctrine of "fair use," although still a bit hazy, permits the use of quotations without securing formal permission when—as a common rule of thumb—fewer than 250 to 500 words are quoted from a full-length work (somewhat less from an article or story). In the case of poetry and lyrics, writers are expected to secure permission for as little as a couplet. The editor will advise the writer which extracts require permission and will also provide, upon request, a form or model letter for making the requests. If the writer uses more than the amounts mentioned, a fee may be levied, which a publisher will generally pay upon publication and charge to the writer's future royalty account.

If the book is an anthology, then the permissions costs should be a priority issue in the negotiations, as they can run from $2000 to as high as $45,000 (the amount estimated in a contract I negotiated for a three-volume history of physics, consisting mostly of extracts). A permissions budget has to be estimated and authorized and should be spelled out in a rider to the contract; the editor will provide some guidelines to help estimate the costs, since permission should not be sought before contracting and before a final table of contents is approved by the editor. This budget, say $4000, is separate from an advance against royalties but is commonly also deducted from future royalties. Be certain that the rider stipulates "from the author's account" or "from future royalties," so that you don't have to reach into your pocket. On rare occasions (and more frequently with textbooks), a writer can negotiate that the publisher assumes half, or even all, the permissions costs—that is, they are not charged to future royalties—but one needs considerable leverage to get this. The editor will tell you whether to secure permissions for North American or world English-language or world rights (successively more costly), and whether for hardcover or paperback or both.

Providing artwork—"all drawings, maps, charts, photographs and all other illustrative material"—is normally the author's responsibility. Many contracts do not specify that the publisher may do so and charge the costs to the author, as this one does. It is nonetheless implicit in a contract, and the details should definitely be negotiated and incorporated into this clause if artwork is expected by the publisher: that is, the specific kind and number of pieces of artwork. Contracts often state that the artwork should be "camera ready," meaning in a form that can be used to make plates for the book (for photographs, this might be 8 x 10 glossies or transparencies). If the cost will exceed, as a rule of thumb, $500 (which may include both permission and preparation costs), then, ideally, a separate budget should be negotiated and incorporated into the contract. The cost of this budget will also be deducted from future royalties. However, some publishers will insist that the writer cover the cost of the artwork out of the advance.

Some publishers will agree to secure the artwork; most won't. It can be a tiresome task, and many writers would probably prefer to have the publisher assume the responsibility, depending on the book and the writer's resources. Sometimes the artwork can be purchased, and sometimes it has to be created. In either case, the writer must know whether the publisher expects simulations or guidelines—rough drawings, photocopies, or even just a list of what is necessary artwork—or camera-ready artwork. If camera-ready artwork is required, the editor will assist in securing it, but it will be fundamentally the writer's responsibility. Writers will want to investigate the approximate or actual cost of providing *professional-*

quality artwork, whether photos, line drawings, or whatnot, *before* negotiating this provision. In most instances, the publisher will expect the author to absorb the cost, although who pays for part or all of it *is* negotiable. What should be negotiated is to have the publisher advance the money, generally payable on submission of appropriate receipts or invoices, and to deduct it from future royalties; that is, from "the author's account." Note the ambiguity in this contract, which says "charge the cost thereof to *the Author*," which should be changed to "the author's account" (there was no artwork required for this particular book).

(c) If in the Publisher's opinion an index is required for the Work, the Publisher will so inform the Author and the Author and the Publisher shall consult on who shall prepare the index. If an index is not prepared by the Author, the Publisher shall have the index prepared and charge the cost therefor to the Author's account.

(d) If the manuscript for the Work as delivered is not satisfactory, the Publisher may request the Author in writing to make designated changes or revisions. If the Publisher requests changes and revisions, the Author shall make them within such time as the Publisher may reasonably request and resubmit the manuscript to the Publisher.

(e) If the Author does not deliver the complete manuscript for the Work within three months of the delivery date specified in subparagraph 2(a) hereof or does not deliver a revised manuscript, if requested to do so, within the time reasonably requested or if the manuscript as originally submitted or as revised is not satisfactory to the Publisher, the Publisher shall not be required to publish the Work and shall have the right, exercisable at the Publisher's discretion, to recover from the Author, and the Author agrees to repay on demand, any amounts advanced to Author hereunder, upon receipt of which in full by the Publisher, this Agreement shall terminate.

(c) *The index.* This clause is written as index clauses *should* be written but generally aren't. They are often vague, don't provide the option to have it done by a professional, or imply or state that if the index is done by an indexer, the author has to reach into his or her pocket to pay for it. However it is worded, it should be negotiated and changed to closely approximate the clause in this contract.

(d) and (e) *Revisions.* These are extensions to provision (a), spelling out the implications. Publishers will expect revisions in a reasonable amount of time, which, depending on the book and the extent of the revisions requested, may be as short as a month or as long as six months. If the resubmitted manuscript is still not satisfactory, or if the original manuscript is late and the publisher declines to give an extension, the publisher usually has the right to cancel the contract. Although this contract permits an automatic three-month extension, most don't (although this amount of time is reasonable and would probably hold up on the author's behalf if a court case ensued).

When a manuscript is late by more than three months, a writer has scant legal grounds for contesting either a cancellation or a request to repay "any amounts advanced." However, the issue of an "acceptable" manuscript is more complicated. Assume that the writer has, in good faith, completed a creditable book and delivered it on time, and that it matches fairly closely the outline or synopsis originally accepted by the publisher. It seems quite unfair, after so much time and effort has been spent to produce the work, for the publisher to demand repayment of the advance (and it would be only the amount paid on signing the contract), even if, in the editor's educated opinion (which is all it is), the work does not meet her editorial standards. After all, almost every book is a risk. If, on the basis of certain materials, the publisher is willing to sign it, and the writer has fulfilled his or her part of the bargain in good faith, then to demand repayment is to reduce a publishing contract to an option: If we like it, we'll take it; if we don't, we won't. Magazine agreements conventionally stipulate a kill fee of about 25 percent of the total agreed on, but this convention doesn't exist in book publishing.

Therefore, it is reasonable to request a provision which states that the writer will repay any amounts advanced "from the first proceeds of the sale of the work to another publisher." (In this contract, the writer had already completed the work, so such a provision was unnecessary.) Publishers resist this provision, but it ought to be a priority, and most will grant it if you hold out for it. Successful writers with leverage are often able to negotiate thus: Under any circumstances, if the book is unacceptable, the author keeps the amount advanced. If your book requires a significant outlay of expense money from your advance, such as for travel or secretarial expenses, then you may wish to further add that, should you not be able to repay from first proceeds (if, God forbid, you are not able to sell the work elsewhere), under no circumstances will you be obligated to return the amount you had to lay out. This addendum to the provision is suggested in those instances in which the publisher insists on a capping date if your first-proceeds provision is accepted. That is, the writer repays from the first proceeds "or within 12 months [between 6 and 18 is the rule of thumb], whichever is sooner." In plain language, this means: If you can't sell it—and so we are confirmed in our assessment—you still gotta pay us back.

What if the publisher rejects your manuscript and does not provide what you feel is sufficient evidence of its unacceptability? Perhaps your editor's judgment is poor or perfunctory, or the editor is now at another house (common nowadays) and the new editor is just unenthusiastic about the book and is looking for loopholes. A reasonable house will respond to this complaint by asking other editors in the house to read it, or by sending it out to an expert in that field (the former with fiction, the latter in nonfiction), although you may have to make a fuss to accomplish this.

What if you feel that the editor's rejection, presumably based on editorial considerations, really masks commercial considerations, such as that stiff competition has emerged, or the topic is no longer "hot"? To forestall this, you may try to insert a phrase that states that if the manuscript is unacceptable "for *editorial reasons*, the writer will repay. . . ." I recently signed a book to be written by the current Mr. Olympia, knowing that the yearly contest would occur even before the manuscript was due. I felt that such a safeguard was absolutely necessary in case he didn't win the contest (he didn't) and some executive at the house concluded that a book by an ex-Mr. Olympia would flop. More books are being rejected nowadays than before and although it is still an infrequent occurrence, I think the possibility is so distressing, and the actuality so painful, that it merits all the space we have given to it. In actual practice, what usually happens? Poorly written books are rejected, they are not sold elsewhere, the publisher duns the author for the advance with threatening letters, the author ignores the letters, and the whole thing fades away (provided the author has received no more than about $5000). There are numerous other scenarios, but they would constitute a book in themselves.

> (f) Any amounts which the Publisher has the right to recover from the Author pursuant to the foregoing provisions may be deducted by the Publisher from the amounts due the Author under any other agreement between the Author and the Publisher.

(f) This provision can be invoked only if and when you have a second book under contract with the same publisher. Let us say that your first book has earned back its advance and is consistently earning about $1000 per royalty period, and your second book is doing equally well. Suddenly, returns for your first book are very heavy, and your next statement shows a negative balance; that is, more books were returned than sold, and so you "owe" the publisher $500. With one book at that house, the writer does not repay the unearned balance; either the book subsequently sells enough copies to balance accounts or the publisher absorbs the loss. With two books, however, this permits the publisher to retain royalties due for the second book to offset the unearned balance of the first.

But what happens if the first book does not earn back its *advance* and the second book does (or vice-versa)? Should the publisher be able to deduct an unearned advance from another book that is paying royalties (or sub-rights income) earned beyond its advance? No, not fair. The advance a writer receives for a book is an amount paid for the blood, sweat, and tears that went into it, which is offset by the risk the publisher takes that the book will earn it back. In point of fact, this is how most publishers apply this clause, but if yours turns out to be one of the few with a severe cash-flow problem. . . . Because this clause is ambiguous, a phrase should be inserted such as "except for unearned advances." In practice, I do not bother with that clause unless and until my client is about to sign up a second book with the same house, at which point I identify and exclude the first book from this clause in the second book's contract. But I don't recommend this practice; it is more prudent to delete this provision. If the publisher resists, then duplicate my practice in your second contract.

EDITING AND PROOFS

3. (a) After the Work has been accepted by the Publisher, the Publisher shall edit the manuscript and submit the edited manuscript to the Author for review. The Author shall review the edited manuscript and return it within the time requested by Publisher.

3. Editing and Proofs. (a) This refers to copy editing and is perfectly reasonable and conventional. Most copy editors improve a book, and most authors are delighted with the changes made in style, grammar, usage, and punctuation, not to mention corrected errors of fact, spelling, dates, and citations (and inconsistencies of time, place, names, and so forth that tend to crop up in fiction). A very few copy editors take too much license in any one of these areas, but rather than work up an ulcer, the writer should merely change back the contested matter—with an occasional and brief marginal explanation where appropriate—and include an unruffled and pleasant note to the in-house editor explaining his or her general position. The author has more leverage than the copy editor. But if the writer is violating "house style" (except for fiction, where the writer has more latitude), such as by not including a comma before the conjunction in a series of three or more, and cannot point to some revered authority—say, *The Chicago Manual of Style*—he or she will probably be overruled.

What about substantive editing—deleting a paragraph or three, or a whole page or section, or restructuring the chapter sequence, or rewriting substantial portions? This first editing task is implicit in provisions (a), (d), and (e), which refer to form, content, and revisions; copy editing is a separate and second round. Since the acquiring editor will first edit the work for substantive problems and confer with the writer about them so that necessary revisions can be made—at which point the writer has the opportunity to argue or disagree with the editor—it is very unlikely that at any later stage the writer will be presented with a *fait accompli,* a disemboweled manuscript that he or she is expected to like or lump (as happens all too frequently with articles submitted to magazines). But if you are nervous about this possibility—since few contracts state, as this one does, that the author shall "review" the manuscript—you can ask to insert a phrase that says that the publisher will not "substantively edit the manuscript without consulting the author," if, of course, such a provision is not already in the contract.

(b) The Author agrees to read, revise, correct and promptly return all proofs and other production materials submitted by the Publisher within the time requested by the Publisher. The Author agrees to pay all charges in excess of 10% of the cost of composition for alterations or additions (other than corrections of printers' errors) which the Author makes in proofs, plates or film after the type has been set in conformity with the edited manuscript returned by the Author. These costs shall be charged to the Author's account.

(b) The next stage, two to three months after going over and returning the copy edited manuscript, is to read and correct galleys (called "proofs," even though the increased use of computer typesetting has introduced the term "the first pass," which few editors employ). Publishers expect a "turnaround" of roughly two weeks, plus mail time, to read and correct galleys. Some authors, more frequently novelists, cannot resist the urge to further polish and refine their work, in the process making enough changes in galleys to markedly increase the typesetting bill (virtually all publishers farm out typesetting). A 212-page book costs roughly $2500 to typeset; if the changes a writer makes cost more that $250 (10 percent), the additional amount will be charged against the author's future royalties (changes in later stages, such as page proofs, are quite costly and mount up quickly). Not only is this fair, but a writer can create headaches for numerous departments in the house by substantially rewriting at the galley stage or later. Delayed production causes a ripple effect too detailed to go into here. Resist the urge. Some contracts do not, as this one does, give the writer a 10 percent leeway or explicitly state that such costs shall be charged to the author's account. If yours does not, you will want to change it to reflect these two stipulations.

NONCOMPETITION

4. (a) The Author agrees that the Work shall be the Author's next book, and that the Author shall not undertake to write another book for another publisher until a complete manuscript for the Work has been delivered to the Publisher.

(b) During the term hereof, the Author shall not publish, or cause or permit to be published, any book on the same or similar subject matter as the Work that would conflict with or lessen its sale.

4. Noncompetition. (a) This clause commits the author to neither write nor contract for another book once the contract is signed. If you have another book *already* under contract—and the contract for it does not similarly restrict your writing via this clause or an option clause—it is necessary only to inform the editor about it (put it in writing before you conclude negotiations): what it is, what stage it is in, and when you expect to complete it. Professional writers sometimes work on two books at the same time, and as long as the writer can meet deadlines, no problems should arise. Some writers sign a two- or three-book contract with the same house. This provision attempts to prevent a writer from signing a second contract with another house before completing the first book, thereby diluting time and energy so that the first book not only doesn't get the writer's full attention but also risks being delayed. If the first house has an option, then signing another contract would thus be a breach of two provisions, unless an exception were incorporated into the contract or added later as an amendment. In practice, nothing prevents the prolific writer from working on a second project so long as a contract is not signed for it until the first manuscript is delivered.

(b) "During the term hereof" means so long as the current book is in print. It is reasonable for your publisher to expect that you will not immediately turn around and contract for another book that would encroach on the sales of the book he paid for. In nonfiction, it is often the case that a writer who is expert in one field—say, real estate or film history—will write more than one book on the same "general" topic. One of my clients wrote a book on buying houses, followed by one on selling houses. Occasionally, the two books may seem, to the lay person (or the editor) to overlap sufficiently so as to represent competition. If the writer can clearly show that they don't, even though the books would appeal to the same audience, no problems should arise. If in doubt, query the editor (this often appears as a provision in this clause). And it may be politic to pave the way by offering that house the book first, even if it does not have an option, provided relations are good and the writer feels that the house is suitable for the next book. The longer a book is in print, and the more modest the dwindling sales, the fewer legal and moral obligations this clause involves. In fact, it is not uncommon to add a phrase curtailing this provision once two, three, or four years have passed.

> 5. (a) If the Author has delivered an acceptable manuscript for the Work and other required materials in accordance with Paragraph 2 hereof and has complied with any requests made in accordance with subparagraph 10.(b) hereof, the Publisher shall publish the Work within   12   months from the date of the Publisher's written acceptance of the Work. Publication shall be in such manner and style and at such price or prices as the Publisher may deem appropriate, it being understood that advertising, number and destination of free copies and all details of manufacture, distribution and promotion shall be at the discretion of the Publisher. If the Publisher fails to publish, or cause to be published, the Work within the period provided herein, for reasons other than first serialization, book club use, delays of the Author in returning the edited manuscript and/or proofs or for the reasons described in subparagraph 10.(b) or Paragraph 15 hereof and if at any time thereafter the Publisher receives written notice from the Author demanding publication, the Publisher shall within 90 days of its receipt of such written demand either publish the Work or revert to the Author in writing all rights to the Work granted to the Publisher herein (subject to any out-

standing licenses which shall be assigned to Author if permitted by the terms of such licenses) and the Author shall retain any advance payments made hereunder prior to such reversion as liquidated damages for the Publisher's failure to publish the Work.

5. Publication.   (a) Many contracts do not have a boilerplate provision committing the publisher to publication within a specific amount of time. A year is optimum for most books, eighteen months acceptable, twenty-four only for lengthy and complicated tomes. Without a specific commitment, the publisher can "bump" your book by a season or two without a second thought if—for a variety of possible reasons—it suits its needs. For instance, a completed manuscript may come in that is both more timely than your book and seems to have more sales potential, or the publisher may decide to cut back next season's list to thirty books from the thirty-five that were planned. Therefore, it is important to insert a provision with a specific time limit for publication. A month's or even a season's delay to allow for a significant first serial publication or book-club sale is reasonable, but not that common, and is in both your best interests, because of the free-publicity value of an excerpt appearing close to publication date, or the larger first-print run a bookclub "run-on" entails. Many contracts further state here that the publisher's responsibility is mitigated by "Acts of God"; that is, strikes, wars, floods, and other catastrophes.

What control or what degree of latitude can a writer exercise over the "manner and style . . ." or prices, design, advertising, and size of the first printing of the book, either informally or by means of inserting provisions in the contract? Well, some of this and some of that, all depending on the writer's leverage. One key issue is whether the book is to be published first in a hardcover edition or a paperback edition, or with the former followed by the latter, both simultaneously, or cloth with the possibility of a paperback, or any of these plus a mass market edition, or only in a mass market edition. If the writer has discussed the publisher's strategy with the editor during the initial negotiation, he or she will learn whether the house's intentions are clear—which is the case most of the time—or whether there is some uncertainty. If the editor and author are in complete agreement—deciding on hardcover followed by paperback within a year to eighteen months, for example—then the author can choose to have this made formal with a provision, which many publishers will accept. However, although the appropriate format is *sometimes* obvious to both parties (this particular book is somewhat esoteric and its limited but easily targeted audience is willing to pay approximately $20 for a hardcover edition, so it was evident to the author, editor, and me what the strategy would be), it often isn't. A literary novel sold to a hardcover house—one that *primarily* publishes hardcovers, such as Morrow and Little, Brown, all of which do have paperback lines but focus on hardcovers—would undoubtedly be published in hardcover first and, depending on the sales and the reception of the book, would either be issued in trade paperback a year or two later, sold for reprint rights to a mass market house, remain in hardcover, or just die a quiet death.

With nonfiction, some genres are invariably published as hardcovers first, such as biographies, and some could go into any format, depending on the house and the editor. The ideal format is sometimes a guess based on savvy and hunch. When the format is a high-priority issue for the writer, who senses some equivocation about it, requesting a provision is reasonable and possible. A guarantee of hardcover publication is possible; a guarantee of hardcover plus a paperback edition within twelve to twenty-four months (with a qualifying provision that the publisher can determine whether to try to sell paperback rights first) is a little less possible. These decisions are often based on events to come, especially the critical reception and sales of the book, and so in many instances the publisher is justified in refusing to commit itself to a specific strategy. Some books are obvious and present no advance decision-making problem, but others aren't. Each writer has to determine how important a priority the format is but should definitely listen to the editor's arguments before taking a strong position. There are individual cases and various reasons for deciding on which format is ideal, but they are too numerous to mention here. The bottom line is that format *is* sometimes negotiable.

However, in the matter of interior design, jacket art, trim size, amount of artwork, color versus black and white, and so forth, publishers are less responsive to author's demands and considerably less willing to incorporate commitments into a contract (unless you have a *lot* of leverage). Having looked at several different examples of that house's recent books, a writer can decide if they look satisfactory and leave it at that; most do. If the issue is more important, a writer can request a provision that permits "consultation" on certain physical properties of the book; many houses will agree to "Author shall be consulted on cover art, catalogue copy, jacket copy and artwork layout" but are unlikely to go further. If the issue is crucial, where artwork or design are integral to the book and might have a clear effect on sales, then a writer has to decide exactly which aspects are crucial and have to be formally agreed on, and where the line is drawn. Lastly there is advertising, which is something of a red herring, since its effectiveness is still considered moot for most books unless the house is prepared to spend an inordinate sum. This is an uncomfortable issue for writers, generally anguished about too little and too late. Very few writers have the leverage to insist on a specific advertising budget. The best one can generally demand is a flyer (this is for nonfiction only) for those books that have an audience clearly targeted and reachable by mail; a book on how to raise teenagers therefore doesn't warrant a flyer, whereas one on quiltmaking or ham radios might. You can and should stipulate a minimum number of copies of such a flyer, which can range from 5,000 to 50,000 or more, and which should be based on specific data that you have researched, such as organization membership or circulation figures. As a rule of thumb, trade publishers allocate 10 percent of a book's estimated first-year income for ads; this formula, alas, is more honored in the breach than the observance.

This clause further stipulates—as most contracts now do—that the publisher's legal damages for failing to publish the book are limited to the advance paid to the author. There have been several cases in the past ten years in which the author sued the publisher for breach of contract for failing to publish the book. Some authors won damages—especially where timeliness was crucial; most didn't. No clear precedent has been set, but the scales are tipped in favor of the publisher who chooses, for whatever reason, not to publish. One reason is that the burden of proving how much income has been lost by the publisher's failure to publish rests with the author; this is obviously very difficult to substantiate, so any damages awarded are likely to be modest. Moreover, litigation is *very* costly, and it may take years for a final judgment to be decreed. If, for whatever reason, the day comes when your publisher does not wish to publish the book, but you have received the second half of your advance, the reasonable course of action is to locate another house. If your publisher has not paid the second half of the advance, precedence and the law are on your side, and the threat of a suit—you may need a lawyer—is usually sufficient to ensure a settlement.

Author's representative 4 copies and
(b) The Publisher shall give the/Author 10 copies of the Publisher's
first edition of the Work upon first publication, and shall at the Author's request, make available further copies at a discount of 50%
from the Publisher's invoice price for the Author's own use, but not
for resale.

(b) *Free copies.* All publishers supply between five and twenty
free copies (of a hardcover; sometimes more of a paperback) and will
sell the author additional copies at an average of 40 percent discount, with royalties paid, or 50 percent, with no royalties paid (this
publisher is more generous than most). If you intend to order more
than fifty copies at a time, you can negotiate a sliding-scale discount
based on your publisher's own "best discount" schedule.

6. The Publisher shall pay to the Author the following royalties on
sales, less returns, of copies of the Work published by Publisher:
(a) on all hardcover copies sold through ordinary channels of
trade in the United States (except as otherwise provided below)
10   % of the invoice price on   the first 5,000 copies; 12½% of
the invoice price on the next 5,000 copies; and 15% of the
invoice price on all copies thereafter.
Invoice price for royalty calculation purposes shall be the price
shown on the Publisher's invoices from which discounts are deducted
to calculate the amounts payable to the Publisher by its accounts and
not the suggested customers' price, if any, printed on copies of the
Work if such price includes an addition to the invoice price to cover
the cost of postage or freight. Notwithstanding the foregoing, royalties
will be calculated on an amount which is no less than 95% of the
suggested customers' price, if any, printed on copies of the Work.

6. Royalties.   (a) The royalty rate of 10 percent for the first 5000 copies, 12½ percent for the next 5000, and 15 percent thereafter is the
most common rate for hardcover trade books at most major houses,
although some, as house policy, pay a lower rate, such as 10 percent
for the first 10,000, and so forth. With sufficient leverage, they may
bend house policy (as in an auction with several houses eagerly
competing for the same book), and a few successful authors demand
and get a rate of 15 percent from copy one. Many smaller houses pay
royalties based on net receipts, even for trade books, in which case
you may be able to negotiate beginning the rate at 12½ percent and
escalating to 15 and then 17½ percent, and/or escalating at steps of
3000 rather than 5000. "Net receipts" refers to the amount that the
publisher actually receives from the wholesaler or bookseller. A

book with a list price of $10, sold at an average discount of 45 percent, results in a net receipt of $5.50. If your royalty is based on net receipts, then in this case you would receive $.55, whereas if it is based on the list price, you would receive $1. Quite a difference! Be sure you know whether your negotiation is based on list price or net receipts. Don't expect a deviation from house policy unless you are in a very strong bargaining position.

In the past five years many publishers have increased their list prices by about fifty cents, in response to demands from booksellers that shipping costs, commonly paid by the bookseller, were cutting too heavily into their modest profits. This increase was added to the jacket price but was not charged (invoiced) to the bookseller, who retained it from the consumer sale free and clear. Publishers, naturally, feel that they should not pay royalties on this fifty-cent raise and during this transition period have asked authors to forgo the nickel or so that might be due them. Virtually all agents and authors agreed, and on most new contracts it is included and binding.

> (b) on all hardcover copies sold in the United States at discounts of 50% or more from the invoice price (including copies sold at such discounts through ordinary channels of trade) and on all hardcover copies sold ~~in school editions~~ as premiums or as special sales or to ~~educational institutions or to~~ others outside the ordinary channels of trade and on all hardcover copies sold in or for the territories or possessions of the United States, for export to Canada or elsewhere throughout the ~~world,~~ territory 10% of the amounts received by the Publisher.

(b) This provision lowers the royalties by about half in a variety of circumstances. For trade books, the publisher's discount schedule—the rate at which copies are sold to retail and wholesale booksellers—generally begins at 40 percent and increases to 50 percent or even higher, depending on the number of copies purchased. Most of the forty or fifty major houses, such as this one, do not go above 48 percent, and this first part of the provision is never invoked. However, many other trade book houses *do* give 50 percent discounts for large quantities, so the key question for an author is approximately what percentage of "normal" sales are made at this discount. For some houses it is as high as 50 to 60 percent of sales. A writer will want to ask the editor this question—you may have to press for an answer; better yet, request the printed schedule—and consider inserting a provision that limits the reduction of normal royalties to no more than 25, 35, 40, or at most 50 percent of the sales of that book. Given a choice between two houses, one of which does give booksellers a 50 percent discount and one of which doesn't, I might be inclined to choose the latter, even if it meant taking a somewhat lower advance. Some houses insert a formula in this provision, reducing the author's royalty by ½ or 1 percent for every additional 1 percent discount given to the bookseller above, say, 46 percent. This is one provision to examine carefully, and be sure to ask about the discount schedule.

"School editions" are very rarely made from trade books, but why chance it? Delete it. The publisher is already protected by the previous high-discount provision. Premiums and special sales—which happen to fewer than one out of one hundred books—are always sold at a high discount, and reductions in royalties are reasonable. A bank, for example, might buy 1000 copies of *How to Invest in Securities* to give away as a premium to customers who open up savings accounts for $1000 or more. Or Chrysler Corporation might buy 2000 copies of Lee Iacocca's autobiography to send as gifts to all of its dealers. The brass ring is the possibility of extraordinary sales of more than 50,000 copies to, for example, a breakfast cereal manufacturer who offers a book in exchange for five coupons clipped from the cereal packages, or a computer manufacturer who gives away a copy of a book on a particular computer language to every purchaser of that computer. In the past five years most of the major trade houses have made more intensive efforts to sell books through these methods.

Export sales are those made out of the country, whether to Canada, the Philippines, or England, and are generally sold in bulk, at high discounts, so that reasonable royalty reductions are fair.

> (c) on all paperback copies sold through ordinary channels of trade in the United States (except as otherwise provided below), 7½% of the invoice price up to 20,000 copies; 10% thereafter.

(c) *Paperback royalties.* These refer to "trade" paperbacks, the larger paperbacks, and do not include "mass market" paperbacks, the smaller, rack-size books such as are found in drugstores, airports, and so forth (this house does not have a mass market division; if it did it would have a separate rate provision for them). The royalty rate here, 7½ percent up to 20,000 copies, and 10 percent thereafter, is about the best a writer can strive for. Unlike hardcover royalties, trade paperback royalties are more flexible and varied in the industry, and "fixed house policy" is usually not as rigid. These rates begin at 5 percent (too low) and go as high as 10 percent, though usually at an escalation after the sale of anywhere from 10,000 to 50,000 copies. The average rate begins at 6 percent and escalates to 7½ after 15,000 to 30,000 copies, but the escalation step varies from house to house and is negotiable. A writer would start with the rate in this contract and fall back where necessary. A three-tiered escalation is negotiable as well: for example, 6 percent up to 20,000 copies, 7½ up to 35,000 (or 50,000), and 8½, 9, or 10 percent thereafter. Any permutation is possible. We will discuss the particulars of mass market, young adult, professional, text, and other division royalties in the chapter on contract variations.

> (d) on all paperback copies sold in the United States at discounts of 51% or more from the invoice price (including copies sold at such discounts through ordinary channels of trade) and on all paperback copies sold in school editions, as premiums or as special sales or to educational institutions or to others outside the ordinary channels of trade and on all paperback copies sold in or for the territories or possessions of the United States, for export to Canada or elsewhere throughout the world, 7½% of the amounts received by the Publisher;   territory
>
> (e) on all copies of any of the Publisher's editions of the Work sold directly by the Publisher to the consumer, such as by mail order or in response to ads sponsored by the Publisher in newspapers or periodicals or on radio or television, 5% of the invoice price;
>
> (f) on all copies of any of the Publisher's editions sold through remainder sales at more than the cost of manufacture, 10% of the amounts received by the Publisher;

(d) Like hardcovers, as discussed in provision (b), paperback royalties are reduced in a variety of situations that call for higher discounts to booksellers.

(e) Virtually all houses pay a royalty of 5 percent based on net receipts (the price given in a coupon ad or flyer) for this category of sales, although some will agree to one-half the *prevailing* royalty rate. The justification for lowering the royalty is that the cost of fulfillment—processing and shipping a single-copy order—is much higher than fulfilling sales made in quantity.

(f) *Remainder sales.* If the book is selling poorly and the publisher decides to let it go out of print, or if a paperback edition is to appear and the publisher has more stock in inventory than can be reasonably expected to sell in the next year or so, part or all of it may be remaindered. That is, inventory will be sold to booksellers at or below the actual unit cost, who will in turn sell the book at anywhere from one-half to one-tenth of the original list price. As the publisher is losing money on these sales, a reduction in royalty is certainly fair. Most houses pay no royalties when books are sold below unit cost. You should add a sentence to this provision that permits you first crack at purchasing as many copies as you want at this low remainder price. This provision is often found in the "termination" clause of many contracts (it isn't in this one), but by inserting it here the writer can buy copies cheaply even if the book is not going out of print but is being remaindered before the appearance of a paperback.

(g) no royalties on any copies of any of the Publisher's editions of the Work given to the Author, given away for publicity or to promote sales or on copies sold at or below the cost of manufacture or on damaged copies or copies destroyed;

(h) only copies sold pursuant to (a) and (c) shall be counted in determining the applicable percentages of graduated sales, if any, set forth in subparagraphs (a) and (c) hereof;

(i) as an advance against royalties and the proceeds from the disposition of subsidiary rights due the Author hereunder, the Publisher shall pay to the Author the sum of $10,000 payable to the Author as follows:

(i) $5,000 upon signing of this Agreement;

(ii) $5,000 upon the delivery of the completed manuscript of the Work, acceptable to the Publisher in form and content.

This provision shall not apply to revised editions of the Work.

(g) This provision is conventional and fair but also contains a niggling ambiguity that a more punctilious agent might question: If the remainder sale provides a 10 percent royalty for copies sold "at or below the cost of manufacturing, "under what circumstances might *this* provision be invoked, and why shouldn't a royalty also be paid? If the book is selling poorly, and the publisher takes a very low offer for the book for a premium or special sale, why shouldn't the author get a modest royalty, just as would happen with remainder sales? Well, agents aren't perfect; on this one I goofed.

(h) Only sales made through normal channels, and at discounts below 50 percent (i.e., excluding export and premium and special sales, etc.), will be counted in determining when the royalties will jump to the next escalation. This is a conventional and industry-wide practice, even though a case could be made against it. Don't fight it.

(i) *Advances*. Aha! The one you've been waiting for. How I wish I could say that this is a simple issue—because if it were, it would remove not a little uncertainty and anxiety from my own life. The larger, the more prestigious, the more glamorous and the more patently successful houses pay higher advances . . . sometimes, but not necessarily, and not as a useful rule of thumb. Generally speaking, the amount of an advance a publisher is willing to pay is directly related to that publisher's guesstimate of first year's sales and potential subsidiary rights income. *Guesstimate* is the key word, for the same book, sent to twenty-five different houses, would produce twenty-five different guesstimates. Of course, they would usually fit into a bell curve and might fall within a narrow median range. If an agent or a writer were to auction a book to ten houses, that house at the very far right end of the bell curve is the one being sought—the house that is willing to pay the most for that book, the house that made the most optimistic guesstimate. In sum, a book's initial financial worth to a publisher (the highest amount it is willing to offer) is a product of that particular publisher's educated fantasy about how much income it will generate for the house in its first year.

For this reason, agents are prone to make multiple submissions and hold auctions, especially when it appears that a book has considerable but hard-to-estimate potential. If I represented Frank Sinatra's autobiography, I might just go to that one among the half dozen most glamorous, high-powered houses that I thought would work most amicably with the author, do the best editing, and promote this kind of celebrity book better than the others. My author would get the $1 million or $2 million that he doesn't need, we could negotiate the ideal contract, and that would be the end of it. For some books— though not-so-obvious bestsellers—a guesstimate of potential sales is relatively easy to make, and most experienced agents' and editors' informed estimates would fall into the same general range. Genre books in particular, whether needlecraft or paperback mysteries, lend themselves to consensual judgment.

To get to the point—let us start with nonfiction—the editor, as a rule of thumb, is generally willing to make a offer based on the computation of potential royalties from the first year's sales. A book with a projected list price of $15 and a projected first year's sales of 5000 copies would yield a royalty of $7500. With a deduction of 20 to

25 percent to account for the return of unsold copies (the industry average for hardcovers; mass market paperbacks average 40 to 50 percent), the editor's highest offer (but maybe not the first offer) will run to about $6000 for this modest book. In practice, many houses will offer no more than $2500 to $5000 for modest nonfiction titles. Subsidiary rights, unless the author already has a track record, are difficult to guesstimate and may not be calculated into the expected first year's revenue. In order to reasonably negotiate with an editor, it follows that a writer first asks for the tentative list price and the estimate of first year's sales. Note that for a trade paperback with a list price of $6.95 and a 7½ percent royalty (roughly $.52 royalty per copy), an editor would have to project sales in excess of 15,000 copies to make a similar offer. Most houses seem conservative in their sales estimates—especially if you discuss this topic with authors—but the proof is in the pudding. Less than one third of the books that are published earn money in excess of the advance. To get this "rule of thumb" advance you will have to negotiate, since few editors will offer that amount off the bat.

Occasionally, two mitigating factors will cause publishers to abandon this rule of thumb. If an editor's enthusiasm for a book is contagious, and other key decision-makers catch the fever—for example, for a first novel—publishers will sometimes pay a higher advance than they realistically feel the book is worth; that is, more than they estimate it would earn in royalties and rights from the first year's sales. On the other hand, some books, by virtue of their length or necessary artwork, or for other similar reasons, will have such high start-up costs that estimated profit margins for the first printing are very small. The publisher will then want to reduce the financial risk by offering a low advance, and perhaps as well a reduced royalty or a royalty based on net receipts for the first printing. Expensive "coffee table" books and art books often pay a 5 percent of list royalty for the first 5000 to 10,000 copies.

On rare occasions, some houses will also pay a certain amount or percentage for extraordinary but necessary expenses, based on your persuasive and itemized list, which may or may not be tacked on to the author's account (this is negotiable). But, generally speaking, the publisher expects your advance to cover *all* expenses, even if it won't, and is not concerned with the amount of work, number of years, tedious hours of research, number of interviews and floppy disks, or fits of anxiety or writer's block that the book will cost the author; they will not be calculated into the offer.

With fiction, the guesstimate depends, again, on the author's track record, whether the book is literary or commercial, whether it is a first novel, whether the format is hardcover, trade paperback, or mass market, whether it is a genre novel (romance, science fiction, and so forth), and whether it is a potential blockbuster (or a "big" novel that weighs three pounds or more in manuscript and also has the potential to sell in large quantities) or a lead title. (In paperback this means it is this month's special, and we are printing and expecting to sell a lot of copies.) Generally speaking, hardcover commercial blockbusters pay highest, followed by lead titles, genre (also known as "category") novels, trade paperbacks, and, lastly, first novels.

Some of this information a writer gleans from the initial negotiation with the editor, and it can be used as a guideline, but the key figure is still projected first year's sales. On the bottom of the totem pole financially is the literary first novel, which usually loses money for the house; $2500 to $5000 is the average advance for the one hundred or so nationally known trade houses, less for the other 1000 or so national trade houses. Next up are genre first novels, which are usually published as mass market originals; here, about $3000 to $7500 is average, whether published in hardcover first or not. Commercial novels (of the kind that Arthur Hailey, James Michener and Ken Follett write) and lead titles for paperback houses may command advances as low as $7500 and as high as $50,000, depending upon the house's guesstimate of sales and rights. Some few go higher, of course, but generally only in auctions conducted by agents.

More could be said about advances, as about a number of clauses, but let us conclude by stressing that roughly 75 percent of advances in trade publishing are below $10,000, 20 percent in the $10,000 to $30,000 range, and no more than 5 percent upward of $30,000. As to the mechanics of payment, most houses pay half the advance upon signing the contract and half upon delivery of an acceptable manuscript, regardless of whether you contract with an outline or a completed—but unedited—manuscript. Of late, more houses are breaking payments into thirds (one-third on signing, one-third on delivery, and one-third on publication), but this is nowhere a fixed house policy and should be resisted, although a writer might agree to one-third on signing, one-third on delivery of half the manuscript, and one-third on delivery of a complete and acceptable manuscript. If you have completed a good part of the work and are running out of money, most publishers will yield to a plea for a portion of the advance due on delivery.

7. The Author grants and assigns to the Publisher the right, solely and exclusively, to exercise, to dispose of or to license the disposition of the subsidiary rights in and to the Work described below, and the proceeds received by the Publisher from any grant of such rights to a third party shall be divided between the Author and the Publisher as specified: *

		Author's Percentage	Publisher's Percentage
(a)	Periodical or newspaper publication prior to book publication;	90	10
(b)	Periodical or newspaper publication following book publication; syndication; publication of condensations, abridgments, selections and in anthologies;	50	50
** (c)	Book Club publication;	50	50
(d)	Publication of editions for premium or special use or for direct sale to consumers through mail order;	50	50
(e)	Foreign-language publication (including the right to sublicense the other rights granted herein to foreign language publishers);	100	0
(f)	English-language publication outside the United States and Canada (including the right to sublicense the other rights granted herein to English-language publishers);	100	0
** (g)	Paperback reprint editions;	50	50
(h)	Hardcover reprint editions;	50	50
(i)	Motion picture, television, radio and live-stage dramatic adaptation rights and allied rights; commercial and/or merchandising and lyric rights, the Publisher to act as the Author's agent for the disposition of such rights and the disposition thereof shall be subject to the Author's approval;	100	0

(j) Non-dramatic audio and/or visual verbatim recordings and non-dramatic audio and/or visual adaptations of the Work or portions of the Work by whatever means made or transmitted, ~~whether now in existence or hereafter invented~~, including but not limited to microfilm, microfiche, information storage and retrieval systems, filmstrip, cassette, disc, tape and wire recording, photocopying, electronic transmission and transparencies ~~and public reading rights;~~	50	50
(k) Braille, large-type and other editions for the handicapped (the Publisher may also grant such rights to recognized nonprofit organizations for the handicapped without charge and without payment to the Author).	50	50
(l) If the Publisher exercises any of the rights described above, the amounts payable to the Author on such disposition shall be subject to mutual agreement, with the exception of those rights for which specific provision is made in Paragraph 6 hereof.	50	50

* All income due the Author from the sale of subsidiary rights shall be paid to the Author within 30 days of receipt by the Publisher, provided the Author's share of such income exceeds $250.00, and further provided the advance as specified in subparagraph 6(i) hereof has been recouped by Publisher and such monies are not applicable to any unearned balance in the Author's account.

** The Publisher agrees to notify the Author's representative about the proposed financial terms, before Publisher accepts such terms, for any license of the subsidiary rights in 7(c) and 7(g). The Author's representative agrees to respond to the Publisher within two days from the time of the Publisher's submission; failure to respond shall be deemed acceptance of said terms.

7. Subsidiary Rights.　　There are eleven rights provisions listed in this clause, and they cover virtually all rights found in trade book contracts, although some contracts lump them together or separate them differently. Agents normally retain, or rather attempt to retain, 100 percent of: first serial, British Commonwealth, foreign translation, performance, and—depending on whether there is a possibility of exploiting them—some or all of the rights lumped together in provision (j), which for convenience we will designate "electronic" rights. Publishers vary in terms of the amount of energy and effort they will expend in attempting to exploit these rights, depending on the individual book and its rights possibilities. As the author's agent for these rights, the subrights department performs virtually the same services an individual agent would and in most instances is no more or no less capable and energetic than an agent. Agents retain rights primarily so that the author can keep the revenue, rather than having it deducted from the unearned advance.

The publisher's willingness to forgo control of some rights depends on the writer's (or agent's) leverage, the chances of licensing a right, how much revenue might be at stake, and the individual publisher's house policy—some are more dogged about retaining them than others. The writer without an agent is invariably better off allowing the publisher to act as agent for most rights, because without the know-how and the proper contacts, the writer will not be nearly as effective an agent. For some of the rights, the publisher uses subagents, who receive commissions varying from 7½ to 10 percent. The writer's goals are to decide which rights, if any, are the most likely to be exercised, to try to negotiate the best possible split in the revenue for these rights, and to be more compromising about the others. Some are conventionally negotiable; others generally aren't. Let's take them one by one and then discuss the two provisions inserted at the bottom after all eleven have been covered.

(a) *First serial.* This is the one right that some writers are more likely to exploit successfully than the publisher, but this is usually true only for the writer who has published fairly widely in magazines (whether fiction or nonfiction), has already established contacts there, and knows which magazines are most receptive to the particular subject. The writer whose specialty is travel, for instance, and who has contacts with a variety of magazines receptive to travel pieces, will probably be more energetic about placing first serial rights than the publisher and should attempt to retain 100 percent.

(Don't forget the advantage of retaining all the revenues.) A publisher is generally willing to submit the book for first serial, even if the revenue potential is modest, for the value to the publisher (and to the writer too) of such a publication is the free publicity, as well as the psychological ripple effect on the house—the sales staff, the publicity department, and so forth. The more rights that are sold, the more the publisher is likely to single out the book as a potential winner, and the more energy and money the house is willing to put out to promote and sell it.

The editor's resistance to giving up first serial will, therefore, in part depend on her being assured that the writer can and will actively attempt to exploit it—an assurance the writer should supply if attempting to retain this right. Writers will additionally need to assure the editor that they will coordinate magazine publication in order to gain the maximum publicity value and impact on sales—that is, no more than one month before or after book publication date. When the house controls first serial, the revenue split varies from 50/50 to 90/10 (as is most common); less than 75/25 is not fair. In some instances, the house may be more resistant to releasing this right; for example, a self-help book that has a strong possibility for placement or even serialization in one of the major magazines, whether *Playboy*, *The National Enquirer*, or *Family Circle*, represents such significant potential publicity (and revenue too) that the house is unwilling to risk losing the publicity.

Newspaper serialization (both first and second) is normally farmed out by the publisher to one of the dozen or so "syndicates" that specialize in submitting the book to a host of major newspapers and newspaper chains. Syndicates—if they agree to buy and represent a particular book—will pay an advance against a 50 percent share of revenue. In other words, if a syndicate takes in $1000 from the sales of newspaper rights, the publisher received $500, and the writer receives whatever share the negotiated split calls for. If a writer retains first serial for magazines, the publisher should be permitted to retain the newspaper rights (just delete "periodical" from the provision, or, if they are lumped together, as they are in some contracts, insert "except for periodicals"). In this contract, there was scant chance of a first serial sale, except placement in professional journals. Since this was more likely to be an unrewarding headache for me than it was a possible sale, I preferred to let the publisher deal with it.

(b) *Second serial.* It is industry-wide practice for the publisher to retain this right for a 50/50 split, and to exploit it for promotion of a book that it hopes is still on the bookstore shelf and selling.

(c) *Book club rights.* Here again, it is industry-wide practice for the publisher to retain this right for a 50/50 split, although a few writers, with considerable leverage, may negotiate a 60/40 or 75/25 split. All publishers automatically attempt to place this right and will submit bound galleys (about three to four months before publication) to three or more appropriate clubs, of which there are close to 200. Only a few books are potential main selections for major clubs, such as the Book of the Month Club or the Literary Guild, where the potential advance against royalties can range from $20,000 to $100,000. More likely is a modest sale to one of the smaller clubs, such as the Nostalgia Book Club (Americana and film) or the Behavioral Science Book Club (psychology).

The value of a modest sale to a publisher is less the advance money than the increased size of the first print run. If a book has a projected first print run of 7500 copies, a run-on sale of an additional 2500 copies to a small club means a first print run of 10,000 copies and a lower unit price per copy (the more copies printed, the lower the unit cost). If the unit price for a $15.00 book is $3.00 with a first printing of 7500 copies, it may be $2.75 for a first print run of 10,000; that $.25 is pure profit, or it may permit the publisher to lower the list price to $13.95. Moreover, any book club sale, or any other rights sale prior to publication, serves to stimulate in-house interest in the book and helps to encourage the sales staff to push that title on their pre-publication sales calls. Selling twenty-five to fifty books a season, the sales people naturally pay more attention to books that appear to be possible winners, which is evidenced by pre-publication blurbs, reviews, and rights sales. Obviously, a book club sale of 10,000 copies has a correspondingly greater impact on the unit price and the net profit. The major clubs, when they run off more than 10,000 copies, may buy duplicate plates from the publisher and print the book themselves, usually on cheaper paper.

Book clubs pay an advance against a conventional royalty of 10 percent of net receipts (smaller clubs sometimes pay lower royalties), with a considerably lower royalty for books used as premiums (of the "three for a dollar" variety). They buy bound copies from the publisher for unit cost or a fraction over cost—from one-fifth to one-seventh of the list price.

(d) This is an extension of provisions 6 (b) and (e) but refers to licensing another firm or publisher to produce copies for premiums or special uses. It is rarely invoked.

(e) *Foreign language rights.* Virtually all houses, as mentioned before, use sub-agents in foreign countries (such agents represent U.S. agents as well as publishers), who receive a commission of 7½ to 12½ percent. Only a small percentage of books are placed, since the cost of translating has to be added to production costs, and a book with modest potential in the United States—say, a 6000-copy sale—becomes too costly in translation even with the same sales potential in a foreign country. Bear this in mind in your negotiation, using your foreign rights share as a bargaining chip to gain something else potentially more likely to occur or more lucrative. Most foreign publishers wait for bound books—except for potential bestsellers—and won't consider outlines, samples, or even edited manuscripts. For this reason, a foreign edition can take two years to appear after a completed manuscript is delivered to a U.S. house. Foreign publishers receive catalogues from U.S. houses (which describe books four to six months before they are published), have "scouts" in the United States, and work directly with the sub-agents in their countries.

Advances and royalties and all other terms are negotiable, as they are here, and very similar to U.S. deals, except for minor deviations from country to country in industry-wide practice. One primary difference is that as the populations are smaller in number, the potential sales are lower than they are for the United States, and so the amount of the advance is correspondingly lower. Just as you grant the publisher the right to license sub rights in the United States, such as first serial and book club, your publisher grants those sub rights for foreign publications, and these are in turn exploited and licensed by the sub-agent.

The common author/publisher split ranges from 50/50 to 85/15; less than 75/25 is not fair (some houses have a fixed policy on this split). This range is equally conventional for the next provision, although 80/20 is the more common split for United Kingdom rights.

(f) *British Commonwealth rights.* A sale is more possible here (although the possibility is still less than one out of fifty), because the work need not be translated, the audience tends to share more common book interests with the United States, and because the U.S. publisher can bring the British publisher in on the print run, which not only lowers the unit price for the U.S. house but also permits it to sell bound copies to the British house at a lower unit cost than would be possible if the British house were to produce the work from scratch. At this writing, the pound is so low that British publishers may choose instead the alternative of buying duplicate negatives (or positives), in addition to which they also pay a modest "offset fee" of $2 to $3 per page, and run off their own copies. The negotiable split is as stated in provision (e). If this right is not licensed *per se*, some publishers will nonetheless distribute and sell export copies in the United Kingdom through their own or a local distributor's office.

(g) *Paperback reprint*. Most reprint sales are made to mass market houses, since so many major trade publishers have their own trade paperback lines and see no reason to license a trade paperback and give up a hefty share of potential profits when they can distribute and sell the book themselves. However, trade publishers can't count on selling mass market rights as frequently as they did five or more years ago, or for as much money, because the mass market houses now issue so many "originals" themselves. With some titles, the publisher has to decide whether a modest reprint sale—say, for an advance under $10,000—is more profitable in the long run than issuing its own trade paperback. With certain genres, such as "category fiction" (romances, mysteries, science fiction, and the like), the mass market profit potential is generally considered greater; with others, the decision is an estimate. In licensing the rights, the publisher has to forgo 50 percent of advances and royalties in favor of the author (occasionally more with writers who have considerable clout). This is just one of several factors that go into the decision. Because choosing to license this right and deciding on a minimum advance is often based on educated estimates, agents (and sometimes authors) like to have the opportunity to put in their two cents' worth. This opportunity can be made formal in two ways: The publisher will either grant "approval" or "consultation" (as in this contract).

With approval, the writer or agent has the right (although it's usually qualified by the phrase "will not be unreasonably withheld") to agree to or reject an offer. Obviously, a writer or agent would need grounds for such a rejection. Recently, a major house submitted on auction one of my clients' novels to ten paperback houses, and it received one offer from a mass market house for a

$3000 advance. Then our approval was sought, since we had this provision in the contract. My advice to my client was to reject the offer, since I felt that such a small advance (of which we were to receive half) meant a very modest commitment from a house that issued 200 mass market paperbacks a year (hence ours was just as likely to sink as to swim). Besides, I said, there were a least ten other paperback houses (mostly non-mass market) that might display a greater interest in the rights. My client agreed, and the book is now out to ten more houses. We risk not being able to revive the first offer if we strike out on this second round, but we felt that it was worth it. Moreover, it is possible that six months or even a year from now an editor at yet another house with a paperback line will read the book and be enthusiastic enough to make an offer for it.

When consultation has been granted, the author or agent has the right to put in his or her two cents' worth, but the final decision rests with the publisher. Obviously, this provision is more likely to be agreed to than approval. Still, getting either one is harder for a writer than for an agent, if only because publishers realize that an agent—who is in the business, knows the ground rules, and is more likely to be dispassionate about a book—is probably going to concur with the house's judgment. The advantage of consultation is having the chance to present a persuasive argument for an alternate course of action if the agent (or writer) disagrees with the house's judgment. My advice would be to request approval but to expect and settle for consultation. When and if the necessity for a consultation arises, have the editor explain the house's position and reasoning, ask for twenty-four hours to sleep on it, and try to consult with a writer (or agent or lawyer or even an editor from another house) who has some experience in book publishing and might raise some points that would not occur to you. The conventional industry-wide split is 50/50, although successful writers with impressive track records are able to improve on this to 55/45, 60/40, or even 70/30.

(h) *Hardcover reprint rights.* This can occur under two circumstances: The house may decide to publish the book as a paperback original and thinks that another house may be better able to exploit limited hardcover sales (of from 1500 to 3000 or so copies). Alternatively, a book that is soon to go out of print might have a continuing sale with a hardcover reprint house (one that specializes in backlist short-run titles—500 to 1000 copies—such as Greenwood, which issues upward of 400 such reprints a year). If either is a possibility, a writer should negotiate an 80/20 or 75/25 split (it was patently not a possibility with this book), although many houses will hold out for 50/50. Both possibilities are long shots, but the former is more likely with a house that publishes mostly paperbacks, such as any of the ten major mass market houses.

(i) *Performance rights* (film, TV, stage, and radio) are here linked with commercial and merchandising rights, although they are separated in most other trade book contracts. Nonfiction usually has a smaller chance of being transformed into another medium than fiction does, but it occasionally happens. Of the small percentage of "properties" that are optioned for a performance right, fewer than 10 percent are actually produced. Since most publishers generally work with performance sub-agents in New York City and on the West Coast and pay a commission to them, a split of 80/20 to 75/25 is fair and common, although some houses will insist on an unfair 50/50. Very few authors have a reason to retain these rights unless they have their own contacts in one of these media, but they should press harder for approval on it, and it is likely to be granted.

"Commercial and merchandising rights" refers to licensing—for example, a paper products company to use some aspect of your work to print on a cocktail napkin, or some character, like one from the "Peanuts" comic strip, on a T-shirt. A few years ago, toilet paper carrying excerpts from books—*The Book of Lists*, for example—was a fad that, thank heaven, seems to have flushed itself away. So few books lend themselves to this right that it isn't worth negotiating better than a 50/50 split if authors encounter resistance unless there is a significant possibility of its use. Few contracts give "approval" in the boilerplate, as this one does, but it is a fair request, as would be retaining 100 percent (many agents do), or at least 75/25.

Incidentally, the reason agents generally retain certain rights, even though there doesn't seem to be a chance of their being exercised (as in this case), or request provisions or riders that don't apply to the work being negotiated, is to set a precedent with that house so that if a future contract is negotiated in which these provisions *might* apply, it is easier—having once negotiated them—to get them a second time. Writers would do well to also keep this in mind.

(j) In my thirteen years as an agent, I have only once had this clause invoked. Of course, that doesn't mean that it might not happen to you. Of late, opportunities are increasing daily, so let us survey it briefly. If your work lends itself to audio or video cassettes or records, you might want to try to retain 100 percent of these rights or negotiate a better split. In any case, you should delete "whether now in existence or hereafter invented," since it is just too open ended. Exercising microfiche or microfilm rights is very rare and will be a very modest source of revenue until libraries dispense with books as they have with old newspapers. Photocopying, because of a very recent court case, has prompted many cautious high schools, colleges, and universities to secure written permission from publishers to photocopy stories, poems, articles, and chapters (the cost of photocopying an entire book is too prohibitive for classroom assignment) when using multiple copies in the classroom. I generally grant this permission *gratis*, as do some publishers, although a modest fee of $10 to $50 might be charged, but I see no point in improving that split. Public readings seem to me an author's right, and I recommend deleting the phrase that restricts them.

Skipping back, the significant possibilities arising from this clause are for computer software and audio or video cassettes. Many computer books have a possibility of software development, as might some few other genres—games, for example, and of late, a few novels, especially mystery and adventure tales. Increasingly, too, audio and video cassettes are being spun off or adapted from books, a market that is likely to grow. Books on Tape, for instance, now offers more than 1000 selections, comprising fiction and nonfiction of both classic and contemporary works. My one experience in this area is with a real estate book, from which a firm wished to adapt the information for a script showing a real estate salesperson going through a house, a co-op, and a condominium to advise homeowners how to best show and discuss the features of each to a potential buyer, what cosmetic changes might be made to increase their value, and so forth. Since the advent of the electronic revolution, publishers are more reluctant to relinquish these rights than hitherto, but the writer who sees any small possibility for an exercise of this right should be able to improve the split to 90/10, 80/20, or 75/25. Few houses will make any effort to exploit these rights, which adds ammunition to the writer's argument to retain 100 percent or to get a better split. Although this book does not lend itself to any of these rights, perhaps I ought to have negotiated a better split.

(k) This provision is found in virtually all contracts. Braille editions (I can't think of any other pertinent handicap) are licensed *gratis*. Large-print editions (mostly best-selling novels, but some nonfiction too) pay a modest advance and royalty but happen to no more than one out of one hundred published books, if that many. I wouldn't bother to negotiate this one.

(l) The last provision in this clause means that if the publisher were to exercise the right, rather than to license it, the terms would be subject to negotiation at that time. An example would be if the publisher started its own book club or mass market division and wished to reprint the writer's book (if it already had either, the contract would contain a separate provision with an agreed-upon royalty). This is also a very unlikely scenario, and as long as the terms are subject to "mutual agreement," I see no reason for changing it.

Inserted provisions. The first inserted provision is known as a "pass-through clause" and means that any of the author's share of the income from subsidiary rights, when it exceeds $250, and *when the advance has been earned out,* shall be paid to the author within thirty days of the publisher's receipt. Here is a common scenario: An author has received a $5000 advance for her book, and prior to publication the house sells first-serial rights to *New Woman* for $1000, so that the author's "unearned balance" has been reduced, by $900, to $4100 (she has a 90/10 split). Shortly thereafter, book club rights are sold to the Organic Gardening Book Club for a $2500 advance, so that her unearned balance is now further reduced, by $1250, to $2850. (In reality, book clubs generally pay half the advance on signing and half at some later point, but let us ignore this fact for the moment.) Her book, with a list price of $15, appears a month later and sells 2500 copies in the first three months, thereby accruing a royalty of $3750. At this point, therefore, she now has earned out her advance and is owed $900, payable when the first statement is sent to her (minus an amount withheld as an advance against returns, which we shall discuss shortly). One week later the British rights are sold to Hodder & Stoughton for £1500, which at today's exchange rate of $1.10 to the pound is about $1650, of which her 75 percent share is approximately $1250. (Are you following me so far?) But of course the British publisher has negotiated paying one-third on signing, one-third on notification from the U.S. house that books have been shipped, and one-third on publication. (If the writer had negotiated approval or consultation she might have pressed her publisher to agree to half on signing and half on receipt of bound books and won her point.) Therefore, of the first check that arrives, her share is $416.33, which her publisher will pay to her within thirty days of receipt. This may seem rather elaborate, but when rights are sold, it is actually a typical unfolding of events.

Was it worth fighting for a pass-through clause to get this check for $416.33 two to five months earlier than it would have arrived, you might well ask? Yes—and here is why. If this author's book was published in January, her first statement would not arrive until October 1, since most houses send statements and checks three (or four or five) months after the semi-annual accounting period, which generally runs from January 1 through June 30 and from July 1 through December 31. In this case she got her check at the end of April, instead of five months later. Moreover, the next two checks for this right will also be sent within thirty days, rather than three months after the accounting period. And what if Dutch rights are sold, then Japanese rights, and then paperback rights? Although it is true that for most books, many rights are not sold, and those for no more than modest sums, one of the key reasons to negotiate the best possible deal is to be as prepared for success as you can. Many publishers will agree to a pass-through clause, although the minimum pass-through amount, here $250, is usually higher. Start with $250 but settle for no more than $1000. With some leverage, writers can negotiate a pass through of first serial, British and foreign rights revenue *before* the advance is earned out.

Consultation. The second inserted provision, linked here by asterisk only to book club and paperback reprint licenses, permits the author (and his or her representative) to have a say in proposed offers, but not a final say (approval). As I mentioned before, it is easier for agents than for authors to get approval or consultation, but it depends on the house's policy and the agent's or author's clout. In this case, I sought approval but had to accept consultation. However, this editor and this house are reasonable—I know from past experience—and would listen to and might be swayed by a reasonable argument were we to disagree on an offer for either of those rights.

In one instance a few years ago, a publisher had a modest book club offer, further diminished by the book club's insistence on paying the second half of the advance a year after its publication (the club pleaded severe cash-flow problems, a term heard quite frequently nowadays in publishing circles). As I then had consultation also, the publisher listened to but did not accept my argument about insisting on having the second half paid sooner. I felt that if the payment schedule were a "deal breaker," the club would agree to it, but the publisher, who did business with this club frequently, was not inclined to put the squeeze on.

As mentioned before, approval or at least consultation of *all* sub rights is worth considering as a negotiation priority. As a fallback position, try to get approval or consultation of some rights in the following descending order: paperback reprint, British, performance, foreign, book club, electronic, first serial, hardcover reprint, premium, commercial. Some agents might mix the order a bit, and it does depend on the particular book, but in most instances the largest potential revenue for a successful book will come from a paperback reprint sale.

8. (a) Accounting of all the Author's earnings hereunder, accompanied by payment of any monies due thereon, shall be rendered no later than April 1 and October 1 of each year, with reference to the periods ending the preceding December 31 and June 30, respectively.

(b) ~~The Publisher may retain a reasonable reserve against returns in any accounting period and shall indicate the amount thereof on the Author's royalty statements.*~~ If the Author receives an overpayment of royalty resulting from copies reported sold but subsequently returned, the Author agrees to pay such amounts to the Publisher and the same may be deducted by the Publisher from any further sums due the Author. Any sums owed by the Author to the Publisher under this Agreement or any other agreement may be deducted from any sum due from the Publisher to the Author hereunder.

8.* (b) The Publisher may retain a reasonable reserve against returns from the amounts due the Author in any accounting period, and the statement issued to the Author for any period for which such a reserve is held shall clearly indicate the amount of such reserve and the statement issued for the subsequent period shall clearly show how the amount previously held has been applied to the Author's royalty account. It is not the intent of this provision that any particular amount be held for longer than the accounting period or that such a reserve shall be held in every accounting period; rather, any reserve held shall be calculated with respect to each accounting rendered, and any reserve shall be reasonably related to the Publisher's reasonable expectation as to returns at the time any statement is prepared. Publisher shall provide, upon request, a detailed explanation of any reserve held.

8. Accounting. (a) Virtually all publishers send out statements and checks within three to five months of the end of the accounting period, but they *always* wait until the last day. Many statements are late, and some publishers need to be reminded that it is overdue. Calendars should be marked to remind yourself that a statement, and perhaps a check, is due. Incidentally, some publishers use a different six-month break (their fiscal year) than the more common January to June and July to December. Most university presses and some professional and small publishers report only once a year. An issue for agents is the amount of data listed—or *not* listed. Few publishers give a complete financial report so that a writer can determine how accurate the statement is. This information includes *numbers of copies printed (and successive reprints); number of copies shipped and sold; type of royalty: regular, special discount, export, etc.; royalty rate for each category; number of copies returned; reserve against returns; and details of subsidiary rights sales and income.*

A request that a full reporting of all these elements be incorporated as a provision into the contract is generally met with stiff resistance. You would be amazed at the variety of excuses and arguments. In practice, agents badger publishers for the missing information after the statement arrives, as should you. If you make enough of a fuss, you will get what you need and will be able to check the figures and spot irregularities. One recent statement I received disclosed a second printing of 12,000 copies, followed by a first of 25,000, indicating 37,000 copies in print, yet the publisher listed sales of only 7000 copies. Why would the house reprint 12,000 copies if it had sold only 7000 copies from the first printing, and presumably had close to 18,000 copies left in inventory? It turned out that the house was holding a huge reserve against returns, and this was not listed on the statement.

    The lesson to learn here is that writers must not only try to protect themselves contractually but also must scrutinize statements carefully and be prepared to question irregularities and raise a stink when appropriate. The squeaky wheel gets the grease.

    (b) *Reserve against returns.* It is now customary for most trade publishers to withhold a percentage of royalties due, against the expectation of returns of unsold books from booksellers, even if there is no provision or clause for it in the contract (although to do so without a provision is, in effect, a breach of contract). When books are shipped by the publisher to bookstores or wholesalers, obviously they have not yet been purchased by the consumer, and a final sale has therefore not yet been consummated. Bookstores generally pay publishers within ninety days of receipt of books, but they sometimes "pay" part of the bill with "returns"; that is, unsold books that they do not think will move off the shelves. Returns for hardcover and trade paperback books run to an average of 20 to 25 percent of books shipped (for mass market books, returns average 35 to 45 percent). It follows that the publisher feels justified in withholding roughly 25 percent of royalties until it is clear—six to nine months later—how the returns are running for your book. This seems reasonable and fair. Note the negotiated addendum (rider 8 [b]), which spells out the concept of "reasonableness" and is about as good a reserve provision as a writer or agent can secure.

Unfortunately, the interpretation of "reasonable" (which is the word found in most contracts) varies considerably from house to house, and many houses abuse this right. They may do it by withholding more than 20 to 25 percent (when there is no indication that returns are running even that high), they may abuse it by retaining the first 25 percent withheld for the next four to six periods, or they may withhold 25 percent from *each* period for the first four to six periods even though total returns over this period do not equal the initial 25 percent.

This abuse is of growing concern to agents and writers, who recognize that these publishers are earning, in addition to thousands of dollars in interest by holding writers' royalties and sub rights income during the three- to five-month lag between the end of the sales period and the issuance of a statement and check, an equal or greater amount of interest by maintaining unnecessary and excessive reserves against returns, often for two, three, or more years. No agent or writer would balk at a *reasonable* reserve, which is sometimes justifiably high for some books that are oversold or overshipped (a common mass market problem).

Agents and writers have failed to make significant inroads into this pernicious system, and until collective action is taken and industry-wide reforms are forced upon publishers, individuals will have to make do with the modest protection given by modifying these provisions as much as possible, and by actively complaining when statements arrive and abuses are noted. Most trade houses have a standard reserve-against-returns policy, which is sometimes flexible and open to negotiation (those for mass market houses usually aren't). During the initial negotiation a writer should ask the editor what the house's policy is and what usually happens in practice (the two don't always coincide). If the answer seems vague or patently unfair, writers should try to negotiate some form of the rider in this contract. One could further request that the reserve be limited to two, three, or four periods, and/or that the amount shall not exceed 20, 25, or 30 percent unless, as herein stated, the reserve "shall be reasonably related to the Publisher's reasonable expectation. . . ." (There are not many elegant writers in the contracts department.)

Some major houses do not report or list on the statement the amount withheld as a reserve against returns. This practice obscures the true sales picture of a book and permits some houses to withhold as much as 65 percent as a reserve without the author's knowledge. Not only is it patently unfair to retain so much of the author's money, but ignorance of the sales figures is detrimental to negotiating another book with the same or another publisher. If a writer's track record is, in fact, much better than his or her statement indicates, then an important bargaining chip is missing. If the amount withheld seems to be high, unfair, or in breach of the provision, you can squawk about it to your editor, who may be willing and able to shake loose part of it. If not, you may have to confront the accounting or royalty department yourself.

> (c) The Author or his duly authorized representative shall have the right, upon reasonable written notice, to examine the records of the Publisher insofar as they relate to the Work during normal business hours and under such conditions as the Publisher may reasonably prescribe. If an error is discovered as a result of any such examination, the party in whose favor the error was made shall promptly pay to the other the amount of the error. Any such examination shall be at the Author's expense unless errors of accounting in the Publisher's favor amounting to 5% or more of the total sum paid to the Author hereunder shall be found, and in such event the Publisher shall contribute to the cost of the examination up to the amount of the error determined thereby.

(c) This provision is *not* found in most contracts, but it is fair and reasonable, and most publishers will accept it (or some house variant thereof) as a rider. Presumably, it helps to keep the publisher honest, although writers and agents very rarely invoke it, and then only where there seems a clear indication that large sums are involved, since it can cost several thousand dollars to hire an accountant to inspect the publisher's accounting records.

How often do publishers play hanky-panky with sales and royalty figures? How often do they *intentionally* report fewer sales of a writer's books than they know have been made? Frankly, I couldn't even guess, and neither could most agents. If a nationally known trade hardcover house were to be caught doing this—when, for example, an agent invoked this provision on the writer's behalf—and it did not seem to be an "honest" mistake, word would get around, since more than half the agents in the United States belong to one of the three agent associations and such information is news. Many agents would then think twice before submitting books to this house. Because major trade houses sign up more than 80 percent of their books from agents, such a reputation would definitely harm the publisher. However, hundreds of publishers are not "major trade houses" and don't rely on agents for most of their books. Moreover, some mass market houses, according to agents, do practice deceptive bookkeeping with sales figures, even though they have already gouged a hefty share of a writer's revenues from their reserves-against-returns practice. Most trade publishers know that only very rarely will a writer or agent invoke this clause. So underreporting does happen, but how often is still anybody's guess.

9. (a) The Publisher shall copyright the Work in the name of ~~John Doux~~ in conformity with the United States Copyright Act and the Universal Copyright Convention, as amended. The publisher is authorized, but not obligated, to take steps to secure copyright in other countries in the Territory and to apply in the Author's name for any renewal of any copyright. The Author agrees that the Publisher may record this Agreement with the U.S. Copyright Office if the Publisher desires to do so and both parties agree to execute at any time all such documents as may be necessary to effectuate copyright in accordance with the provisions of this Agreement.

(b) If the Publisher supplies at the Publisher's expense any textual or illustrative material for the Work, such material may be copyrighted separately as the Publisher shall deem appropriate.

(c) All references to copyright in this Agreement shall reflect any amendment made subsequent to the date of this Agreement in the copyright laws of the United States, in any international copyright convention or in the copyright laws of any other country within the Territory.

(d) In the event of any actual or threatened infringement of the copyright to the Work, the Publisher may employ such remedies as it deems advisable to protect the copyright. The Author hereby authorizes the Publisher to make the Author a co-plaintiff with the Publisher in any litigation which the Publisher may commence to protect the copyright. The Publisher shall bear the entire expense of such litigation. Any recovery therefrom shall be applied first to reimburse the Publisher for its expenses and the balance, if any, shall be divided between the Publisher and the Author as follows: that portion which is based on actual damages shall be divided in proportion to the losses from such infringement suffered by each and that portion which is based upon the infringers' profits or punitive damages shall be divided equally.

(e) So that the Publisher may comply with the requirements of the U.S. Copyright Act, the Author shall notify the Publisher immediately if the Author makes a disposition of rights reserved by the Author which would permit publication of the Work or any portion of the Work prior to the publication of the complete Work under this Agreement. The Author shall promptly deliver to the Publisher two copies of any such prior publication and, if requested to do so by the Publisher, the Author shall also deliver to the Publisher legally recordable assignments to permit the Work to be copyrighted as provided herein.

9. Copyright. The new copyright laws, passed by Congress in 1976, offer excellent protection to writers. The writer "owns" his or her work from the moment it is put on paper and need not register prior to submitting or selling it to a publisher. Publishers (and others) may take a writer's idea and have someone else execute it, because only the "expression" can be copyrighted, not the idea or concept, but in my experience this is not in the least bit common, and few agents or writers need be paranoid about having an unusual idea stolen by an editor or publisher. What does occasionally happen is that, having failed to secure a book on a hot topic, either by making too low an offer or in an auction, an editor may find and commission another writer to write a similar book. Or a good idea is so poorly executed that its chances of being signed up are minuscule, and an agent or editor may have few qualms about "borrowing" it.

Almost all trade publishers will agree to copyright the book in the name of the author, and all authors should request it. The reasons for this are technical and rarely invoked, but why take a chance? The reasons are several: If rights revert to the author under the bankruptcy, default (clear breach of contract), or out-of-print provisions, the writer will not have to pursue or sue for the copyright. (Without clear title to the copyright, a writer cannot relicense to another house.) If the work is out of print but the writer has not formally regained the rights (this will be discussed in the termination clause), most other publishers will seek out the copyright holder to buy or license any rights. If there is a violation of copyright after the book has gone out of print (for example, someone plagiarizes the work, or a foreign country translates and prints it without securing a license), bringing suit can be complicated and difficult without clear title to the copyright. In sum, insist on it.

(a) Publishers will invariably take the responsibility for securing copyright in the United States—and other countries, if rights are sold there—but "renewal" is no longer necessary, because copyright for books published after January 1, 1978, automatically extends to fifty years after the death of the author.

(b) If the publishing house supplies any substantive materials at its own expense, they may be copyrighted in the publisher's name.

(c) Self-explanatory.

(d) The publisher will take the responsibility of protecting any infringement of the copyright and will pay any expenses necessary to do so. After such costs are deducted, the publisher will split with the author any money received for damages.

(e) If a writer sells first serial rights, or any kind of right that is exercised *prior* to book publication, the publisher must be notified and must be sure that the writer has properly protected the copyright of the work. For the details of first-serial protection, refer to the discussion of copyright in the first chapter.

> 10. (a) The Author represents and warrants that the Author is the sole author of the Work; that the Work is original, has never before been published in whole or in part in any form, is not in the public domain in any country included in the Territory and does not infringe upon any copyright or upon any other proprietary or personal right; that the Work contains no matter which is libelous, in violation of any right of privacy, harmful to the user or any third party so as to subject the Publisher to liability or otherwise contrary to law; that the Author is the sole and exclusive owner of the rights herein conveyed to the Publisher and that the Author has not previously assigned, pledged or otherwise encumbered the same; and that the Author has full power to enter into this Agreement and to make the grants herein contained. The Author shall indemnify and hold the Publisher harmless from any loss, damage, expense (including attorneys' fees), recovery or judgment arising from or related to any breach or alleged breach of any of the foregoing warranties. If any claim, demand, action or proceeding is successfully defended, however, the Author's indemnity shall be limited to 50% of the costs and expenses (including attorneys' fees) incurred by the Publisher in the defense thereof.

10. Warranty. (a) A book, or at least a chapter, could be written about this complicated and potentially troublesome clause, found in all contracts, so I will try to stick to the essentials. In the first four lines the writer avows that the work is original (not plagiarized), has not been published previously (or if it has, that the copyright has been protected), and that it doesn't infringe on someone else's rights. For example, a writer cannot use excerpts from personal letters or diaries, even if unpublished, without express permission, unless they are in the public domain (exist more than fifty years after the creator's death). Furthermore, the writer avows that the work is not libelous, does not violate any rights of privacy, and would not be harmful to any "user" (recommending use of the seed in peach pits, which contains cyanide, as flavoring in a peach cobbler recipe in your cookbook might invoke this clause via a suit from a sick and dissatisfied user). Libel and invasion of privacy remain controversial issues in all the media and are too complex to explore here. See the Recommended Reading list to find current works on this topic.

The writer further avows that the material is truly his or hers (did a collaborator help with some of the writing, for example?) and has not been promised elsewhere (is the writer violating an option provision of a contract with a previous publisher?). Now comes the heart of the provision: Namely, if a suit is brought against the writer, it is agreed that the writer, and not the publisher, shall be solely responsible for the consequences (damages awarded, for example) and the legal expenses of defending the suit, *whether the plaintiff's judgment is upheld or not*. In other words, even if a nuisance suit is dismissed, or if the publisher wins the suit on the writer's behalf, the author is still responsible for at least half the costs. Most publishers are very sticky about this clause and will rarely modify it, especially with a controversial book, to suit an agent's or a lawyer's notion of a perfectly fair clause.

The ideal changes to negotiate for are (1) that the author's responsibility be limited to judgments that are "upheld" (the writer was found at fault in a court of law), which is infrequently agreed to, (2) that the publisher not settle a claim or suit out of court without the author's consent, and (3) that the author has the right to choose an attorney to co-defend the claim or suit.

Don't dismiss this provision by assuming that your book *obviously* doesn't apply, since it is one on how to make trout lures. Almost any book has the potential to provoke a claim, since any nut can bring suit on almost any grounds, apparently ridiculous or not, if he or she can afford to pay the filing fee. An encouraging development in this thorny thicket is that in the past three years, more than two dozen major houses have agreed to provide libel insurance for their writers, and more will continue to in the future. This insurance contains a deductible provision, so that writers may be responsible for the first $2500 to $25,000—depending on the individual policy— of any settlement or upheld claim. But when judgments can easily exceed $100,000, such numbers begin to seem like petty cash. With a "hot potato," a book that could easily incur a suit, such as an unauthorized biography of a living notable, writers may wish to first submit to those houses that have such insurance (although you wouldn't want to point out that that is your reason for submitting there!).

Another positive element is that claims and even nuisance suits are relatively rare (although they've grown in number in recent years). In addition, publishers, in practice, tend to protect the author at their own expense if the claim or suit is patently ridiculous or unfair. Finally, for the writer who senses that the work may lend itself to a legitimate suit (writing an unauthorized biography, for example), libel insurance is available at a cost of roughly $3000 for a book (your publisher can provide the names of insurance companies).

(b) If in the opinion of the Publisher there appears to be a substantial risk of liability to third persons or of governmental action against the Work (including, without limitation, actions on the ground that the Work contains obscene matter), the Publisher may have the Work read by the Publisher's counsel at the Publisher's expense. If the Author fails to make or to authorize the Publisher to make such changes or deletions as are recommended by the Publisher upon the advice of the Publisher's counsel, the Publisher may recover from the Author and the Author agrees to repay on demand any amounts advanced to the Author hereunder upon receipt of which in full by the Publisher, this Agreement shall terminate. If the Author agrees to make such changes, and, notwithsanding such changes, there still appears to be a substantial risk of litigation and/or governmental action, the Publisher may terminate this Agreement by written notice to the Author and, in the event of such termination, amounts advanced to the Author by the Publisher shall be repaid by the Author to the Publisher out of the first proceeds received by the Author from any subsequent dispositions of rights to the Work which are subject to this Agreement. If the Author agrees to make changes in the Work as recommended by the Publisher upon the advice of the Publisher's counsel, and if the Work is then published, the Author's indemnity with respect to any judgment shall be limited to 50% to the extent that such judgment arises from a matter within the scope of the Publisher's review and as to which the Author has made full disclosure to the Publisher.

(c) Either party shall, with reasonable promptness, apprise the other of any claim, demand, action or proceeding respecting the Work. The Publisher shall defend any such claim, demand, action or proceeding made against the Publisher with counsel of the Publisher's selection and the Author shall fully cooperate with the Publisher in its conduct of the defense thereof. The Publisher, if it deems advisable, and after consultation with the Author and serious consideration of any objection to settlement which the Author may make, shall have the right to make a settlement of such claim, demand, action or proceeding made against it. The Author and the Publisher shall agree on the percentage of the costs of any such settlement which each shall bear. Failing such agreement, the Publisher shall retain any remedies available to it based on the Author's breach of any warranty or representation made by the Author in this Agreement. Notwithstanding the foregoing, the Author may, in the Author's sole discretion, undertake to hold the Publisher harmless from the further costs of defending any such claim, demand, action or proceeding by providing such security as may be reasonably acceptable to the Publisher, in which event the Publisher shall not settle any such claim, demand, action or proceeding without the Author's consent.

(d) If a judgment against the Publisher results from any claim, demand, action or proceeding, the Publisher shall be under no obligation to appeal any such judgment unless the Author provides the Publisher with security acceptable to the Publisher for the full amount owing to the Publisher because of such judgment and for the further costs and expenses of an appeal.

(e) In the event of any claim, demand, action or proceeding asserting or alleging any matter which, if established, would constitute a breach of any of the Author's representations and warranties, the Publisher shall have the right to withhold a reasonable amount of payments due to the Author under the terms of this Agreement as security for the Author's obligations as stated herein. The Publisher shall deposit any monies so withheld in an interest-bearing account pending disposition of the claim, demand, action or proceeding, and such monies and the interest thereon will be applied first to satisfy the Author's obligation to indemnify the Publisher, and any balance remaining thereafter shall be remitted to the Author promptly after such disposition.

(f) The Publisher shall have the right to extend the Author's representations, warranties and indemnities to third parties (including licensees of subsidiary rights granted to the Publisher herein) and the

Author shall be liable thereon the same extent as if such representations, warranties and indemnities were originally made to such third parties by the Author. The representations, warranties and indemnities set forth herein shall survive in the event this Agreement is terminated.

(b) The publisher will undoubtedly secure, at its own expense, a "libel reading" by an attorney specializing in these matters if there seems to be any risk at all (i.e., won't wait for "substantial risk"). The writer will be expected to make reasonable changes or forfeit the contract and return the advance. It is unlikely that, should such changes be made, the book would still represent a risk sufficient to cause the publisher to back out. Any book this "hot" would have had a red flag attached to it when first submitted, and considerable discussion of the possible consequences would have taken place before an offer was made. In any case, this provision seems perfectly reasonable to me but doesn't, in fact, appear in most contracts.

(c) As suggested in provision (a) of this clause, the author should ideally be able to "approve" any settlement, whereas here "consultation" is given, and the sharing of the expenses is to be agreed on at that time. If you *don't* agree with the publisher's decision, it can avail itself of any remedies the author is committed to by previous sections of this clause (repaying advances or coughing up costs), *if* an actual breach on the author's behalf has been committed (e.g., if you did plagiarize or libel someone). Furthermore, the author can persuade the publisher not to settle out of court, but to continue to the bitter end, provided that the author is willing to put up sufficient "collateral" to cover the estimated future costs (ideally this would be from royalty or rights money due but might have to come from the author's pocket).

(d) If the publisher—on the writer's behalf—loses the case, the publisher is not obligated to appeal the judgment unless the writer puts up collateral to cover the cost of appeal *and* the judgment.

(e) If a claim or suit is brought against the writer, any moneys due, whether from royalties or rights, will be withheld in an escrow account until the matter is concluded, and such moneys will be applied against any costs or settlements due the publisher, following which the author will promptly get a bill for the balance due.

(f) If the publisher licenses a magazine, British publisher, or some other firm to exercise any of the rights granted in the contract, your warranty extends to these license holders. If the agreement is terminated—say, rights are returned to the author three years after publication, when the book goes out of print—but a claim or suit is brought against the publisher in the fourth year, the writer's legal responsibilities survive the termination.

If you are still with me on this clause, you will be relieved (or dismayed) to know that very few houses spell out the warranty clause in such detail. Moreover, as boilerplate clauses go, this one is quite fair (the shorter they are, the worse they are for the author). If a writer's book seems to lend itself to invoking any provision of the "Warranty and Indemnification" clause, as this is usually labeled, it is worth the expense to hire an attorney to review and negotiate it on the author's behalf, even if the author represents him- or herself for the balance of the contract.

> 11. (a) If the Publisher informs the Author in writing that a revised edition of the Work ("revised edition") is necessary, the Author agrees to deliver to the Publisher a manuscript for said revised edition, satisfactory to the Publisher in content and form, at such time as the Publisher may reasonably request. The Author and the Publisher agree that all of the rights and obligations of the Author and the Publisher with respect to the Work shall apply to a revised edition as if it were the Work being published for the first time under this Agreement.
>
> (b) If the Author is unable to prepare a revised edition or does not prepare a revised edition within the time reasonably requested or does not prepare a revised edition for any other reason, the Publisher may arrange for the preparation of a revised edition by parties of the Publisher's selection ("the Revisors"), subject to the Author's right to approve the selection of the Revisors and the content of any revisions prepared by them prior to publication thereof. The Publisher shall determine how much to pay the Revisors, and the amount paid, whether a fee or royalty, shall be deducted from royalties payable to the Author under this agreement and the Publisher shall decide what credit to give the Author and the Revisors in connection with the publication of such revised edition.
>
> (c) The provisions of this Paragraph 11 shall apply to the first and all subsequent revisions of the Work which the Publisher considers necessary.

11. Revised Editions. (a) A few nonfiction trade books have a second life in revised editions, whether in hardcover or paperback. A publisher will request a revision only if the sales figures warrant it (the expectation of selling a minimum of about 2000 copies a year for hardcover and 6000 for paperback, assuming that sales of the first edition steadily diminish from year to year) and the book lends itself to a revision, such as a political history of Mexico. If a book might lend itself to a revision, an appropriate insertion to this clause would be a provision to pay the writer an additional advance against royalties for the second and subsequent editions. This might read: "Publisher agrees to pay a reasonable advance against royalties to prepare a second and subsequent revised editions." Since one doesn't know how many years in the future the revision might be requested, it would be detrimental to suggest the actual sum. If the first edition was successful and the royalty rate modest—say, 6 percent for a paperback—the writer can usually persuade the publisher to increase the rate for a second edition when the time comes. Even without the insertion, most houses would agree to pay an additional advance against royalties if the writer pressed for it. Incidentally, virtually all contracts stipulate, as the last sentence of this provision implies, that royalty rates revert to the same terms as the original—that is, they begin at 10 percent.

(b) This provision, as written here, is unusual in that the boilerplate states "subject to the Author's right to approve the selection. . . ." Most revision clauses do not contain this, but a writer should request it (and why not "the right to select the revisor, subject to the publisher's approval"). As for the "fee or royalty," the writer should insert "subject to the Author's approval, which shall not be unreasonably withheld." Some contracts designate the percentage of royalties that the selected revisor will receive. A fair percentage is 25 percent for the first revised edition and 50 percent thereafter, whereas some contracts start with 50 percent and may go as high as 75 percent.

(c) Self-explanatory.

OPTION   outline and one sample chapter

12. The Author agrees to submit the/manuscript for the Author's next book-length work to the Publisher before showing it to any other publisher, and the Publisher shall thereupon have 30 days to advise the Author whether it wishes to publish the said work and upon what terms. If the Publisher fails to so advise the Author within the specified period, or if the Publisher wishes to publish the said work but is unable within 30 days of its so advising the Author to reach agreement with the Author as to the terms of publication, the Author shall be free to submit said work elsewhere, provided that in the case of

failure-to-reach-agreement-as-to-terms,-the-Author-shall,-prior-to-the-
acceptance-of-a-bona-fide-offer-from-any-third-party,-submit-the-fi---
nancial-terms-thereof-to-the-Publisher-in-writing,-whereupon-the-Pub-
lisher-shall-have-three-working-days-to-advise-the-Author-that-it-will-
publish-the-said-work-on-such-financial-terms-in-which-event-a-con-
tract-will-be-entered-incorporating-all-such-terms-and-the-other-terms-
and-conditions-provided-for-herein.-The-provisions-of-this-Paragraph-
12-shall-survive-the-termination-of-this-Agreement.-

12. Option. An option clause is found in all contracts, with varying degrees of restrictiveness. The wording of the clause should definitely be a priority issue for a writer. The ideal option clause is none
at all, and some publishers will agree to this, depending on the writer's leverage and track record. However, it's harder to get this clause
deleted with fiction than with nonfiction. The first fallback option
clause is the one negotiated here: It gives the publisher first crack at
the book, based on an outline and one sample chapter (no writer
would want to agree to have to wait until the entire manuscript is
completed), on "terms mutually agreeable" (this is the wording to
insert in a contract that doesn't have some such appropriate
phrase), within thirty days of submission. This is, in fact, a "right of
first refusal," not an option. In strict legal terminology, an option is
the right to buy something for a specific price, already agreed on;
publishing contracts often employ the term loosely.

Some other common boilerplate provisions to watch out for
and change are an option "on the same terms as herein stated"
(locking the writer into an advance appropriate in 1985 but perhaps
poor in 1988) and a "matching option" clause, which states that if
the author is dissatisfied with the offer and goes elsewhere, the original publisher has the right to contract the book on the same terms
offered by the other house.

A variant of this provision is a matching option plus 10 percent, meaning that the original publisher can take the book if it increases the other house's offer by 10 percent. Beware of a provision
that states that the publisher does not have to exercise the option until the first manuscript is published. Clearly, this means that the
writer may have to wait as much as a year or more before contracting
with the publisher or with any other house, so this is definitely a
provision to insist on deleting. One alternate position is to give a
right of first refusal only on the writer's next book in the same genre,
or the writer's next book of fiction or nonfiction (freeing the other
category).

Some houses are relatively flexible about their option clauses; others are more rigid about "house policy." Some contracts contain an option clause that is quite complicated or obscure, and writers should insist on a comprehensible interpretation. The provisions of an option clause are crucial, and in those contracts that contain particularly heinous ramifications, such as waiting until the first book is published, or publishing it on the same terms as the first contract, the writer might do well to consider the need to change them as "deal breakers."

TERMINATION

13. (a) If the Work shall be out of print and the Publisher receives from the Author a written request for a reversion of rights, the Publisher shall within six months of its receipt of such request do one of the following: (1) declare in writing its intention to reissue an edition of the Work under one of its imprints; or (2) enter a license providing for the publication in the United States of a new edition of the Work; or (3) revert in writing to the Author the rights granted to the Publisher herein. If the Publisher declares its intention to reissue the Work and does not do so within nine months from the date of its receipt of a request for reversion, all rights granted to the Publisher herein shall automatically revert to the Author. Any reversion pursuant to this Paragraph shall be subject to any grant of rights made to third parties prior to the date of the reversion and the right of the Author and the Publisher to participate in the proceeds therefrom.

(b) The Work shall be deemed out-of-print if no edition of the Work is available in the United States from the Publisher or a licensee of the Publisher and there is no license in effect which provides for the publication of an edition of the Work in the United States within 18 months from the date of such license.

13. Termination. Most contracts contain a termination or out-of-print clause, but for those few that don't, it is important to add such a rider. The boilerplate provisions herein are quite fair and set the standards a writer should request.

(a) Note the vague wording of the first phrase (it's even more vague in some contracts), which requires the *author* to determine whether the book is in print. Virtually all contracts imply or state this, and more often than not, publishers will *not* formally (or even informally) notify a writer that the work is going out of print. The first sign may be a royalty statement containing negative sales (more returns than orders). At this point the writer is advised to take the following steps, rather than to make a telephone call, which may not yield a definitive answer. Write to the publicity department to ask for a current catalogue to see if the book is still listed for sale; check the current *Books in Print* (and don't forget the "Forthcoming Supplement") to see if the book is still listed; and write to the customer service department to order five copies of the book. If all three ploys yield satisfactory results, the work is still in print (which may also be the case if the book is available from a licensee, such as a mass market house).

However, even if the first two tactics prove satisfactory, the writer may receive an invoice stating that the book is "TOS" (temporarily out of stock) or "OSI" (out of stock indefinitely). Some publishers, with no immediate intention of reprinting a book, continue to list it and reply to all orders with a TOS or OSI invoice, waiting to see how many orders pile up, and in what quantities. As this provision normally gives the publisher six months within which to make the decision—which is an adequate amount of time for any publisher to determine whether to reprint a book—the writer will want to request a reversion of rights at the moment he or she divines or even suspects that the work is not available for sale or is out of print.

The main reason for reclaiming the rights, even if the book is no longer selling ten copies a year, is that a writer never knows when some other publisher may be interested in reprinting it. Or some other medium may wish to license any right at all that the writer has granted to the publisher. If the book is not available for sale, then the publisher should not have the right to share in any revenue that might come from a future publisher or licensee. If the writer does *not* reclaim the rights, the publisher will share the revenue from any future sale or license at the rate already stated in the contract.

Note the stipulation that the reversion is subject to any grant of rights made to third parties. In other words, if the book is no longer in print but is used in some other way— perhaps a chapter continues to be reprinted in an anthology published by some other house, or the work has been adapted for performance—the publisher will continue to share in those revenues even if the writer reclaims the book publishing rights.

(b) This provision is not found in most contracts but should be added, because it not only defines what "in print" means but further states "in the United States." A writer would not want the existence of a foreign edition to interfere with the right to reclaim U.S. rights. Eighteen months is too long to have to wait for a reprint of the writer's work; I should have attempted to change this to six, nine, or twelve months.

One common termination provision to watch out for and delete states that the work is still in print if the publisher has given some other publisher an "option" to reprint the work. An option costs the original publisher nothing and could be extended forever, but it has no benefits at all for the writer. Bear in mind that a publisher has nothing to gain by letting rights revert to the author and will, as a matter of policy, attempt to keep them with varying degrees of tenacity. In too many instances publishers retain the rights by default; that is, if the author does nothing, as is generally the case, the publisher retains all granted rights.

RESERVED RIGHTS

14. All rights not granted to the Publisher herein are reserved by the Author. However, the Author shall not license or otherwise dispose of any such rights so as to compete with the rights granted to the Publisher herein or without reserving to the Publisher the rights granted herein. If the Author has reserved periodical and newspaper publication rights prior to book publication, the Author shall not without the consent of the Publisher authorize or permit the publication in newspapers or periodicals of more that 20% of the Work, nor any condensation of the entire Work. If the Author has reserved motion picture, television, radio or live-stage dramatic adaptation rights, the Author shall not in connection with the disposition of any such rights make any grant of publication rights without the Publisher's written approval and shall in no event make any grant of novelization, photonovel, comic book rights or similar rights.

FORCE MAJEURE

15. The failure of the Publisher to publish or reissue the Work shall not be deemed to be a violation of this Agreement or give rise to any right of termination or reversion if such failure is caused by restrictions of governmental agencies, labor disputes or inability to obtain the materials necessary for its manufacture or occurs for any other reason beyond the Publisher's control; and in the event of any delay from any such cause, the publication date or reissue may be postponed accordingly.

GENERAL PROVISIONS

16. The Author shall keep at least one copy of the manuscript for the Work and any other materials submitted to the Publisher hereunder. The Publisher shall, upon the Author's written request made within a year after first publication hereunder, return to the Author the copy of the manuscript used for typesetting; the Publisher shall not be required to retain such manuscript at any time thereafter. The

Publisher shall not be responsible for the loss or damage to any manuscript or any other materials submitted by the Author except in the event of its gross negligence.

17. No advertisements (other than advertisements for other publications of the publisher thereof) shall be included in any edition of the Work published by or under license from the Publisher without the Author's consent.

18. The Author grants to the Publisher the right to use the Author's name, likeness and/or biographical data on any editions of the Work or portions thereof published by the Publisher and in any advertising, publicity or promotion for the Work prepared and disseminated by the Publisher. The Author further agrees that the Publisher may extend this right to any licensee or purchaser of any of the rights granted to the Publisher herein.

14. Reserved Rights. This clause is not found in most contracts, and writers should add the first sentence, by means of an asterisk, to the bottom of the clause in the contract that delineates the various sub rights and the author/publisher split. One never knows what new right may develop in the future.

The second provision herein is self-explanatory.

The third provision, relating to first serial rights (usually found embedded in another clause in some contracts), should have been changed to 50 percent, which seems fairer. Up to a point, however, the publisher would probably consent to extensive serialization on the grounds that the free publicity would help to sell more copies.

The last provision, related to performance rights, seems superfluous to me because these are explicitly or implicitly covered by other clauses in this and most other contracts.

15. Force Majeure. This is not found as a separate clause in most contracts, but is normally embedded in the "Publication" clause (#5 in this contract, where we have already discussed it). Many publishers label events beyond their control "Acts of God."

16. General Provisions. This clause or a variant thereof, is found embedded as a provision in most other contracts and requires little elaboration. A writer who supplies artwork of any kind, such as glossy photographs, that might be difficult, costly, or impossible to replace should notify the editor that as soon as plates are made, the artwork should be returned by messenger or registered and insured mail or, ideally, will be picked up in person. Materials do sometimes go astray or disappear.

17. No Advertisements in the Work.   This clause is not found in most contracts, but the writer who would object to ads appearing in his or her work might want to insert it as a rider. For a while, several years back, ads were sometimes found in mass market novels, but the practice has almost disappeared.

18. Use of Author's Name and Likeness.   This clause is also generally a provision in some other clause. Publishers won't insist on using a photograph if the writer objects, but they will as a matter of course use biographical material on the jacket, in the catalogue, in publicity material (the press release, for example), and perhaps in ads. If you are sensitive to a possible abuse of this privilege, you may insert a phrase that gives you the right to review any such use and to delete possibly objectionable material, such as "She now lives with her wealthy fifth husband in a sprawling Gothic mansion in Malibu."

> 19. (a) If the Publisher is required by law to withhold and pay to any U.S. or foreign governmental taxing authority any portion of amounts due the Author hereunder, such payments shall be deducted from the net amounts due the Author hereunder.
> (b) If any foreign taxes, bank charges or agents' commissions are imposed on any payments due the Publisher from the exercise of any right granted herein, the appropriate allocation of proceeds between the Publisher and the Author from the exercise of such right shall be made on amounts received after such charges have been paid.

19. Taxes.   (a) At this writing, there are no regulations that require a publisher to withhold moneys for taxes for a U.S. citizen, but a situation might arise in which a publisher is authorized to do so—for example, if a lien or garnish of some kind were attached to an author's income. When foreign rights are sold or licensed, many countries require that a U.S. citizen fill out a tax form in order to receive moneys intact. (For a British sale, a copy of this form must pass through the hands of the Internal Revenue Service to insure that a writer declares this income.) When these rights are exercised by the publisher, who receives the revenue directly from any foreign country, the publisher processes any requisite forms. The writer who represents him- or herself, or is represented by an agent, is obliged to fill out and submit this form to avoid double taxation. This is true for countries that have reciprocal tax treaties with the United States, as most Western countries do. Some countries, such as Israel, do not have such treaties with the United States, so their citizens who have books published here must pay double taxes (currently, a stiff 30 percent U.S. tax plus a high Israeli income tax). Conversely, a U.S. author has only 10 percent of moneys deducted from a book published in Israel. But some countries, even those with reciprocal tax treaties, deduct a certain percentage from U.S. writers for taxes. France and Japan—which deduct 10 percent—come to mind.

(b) It seems fair to share the cost of any foreign taxes or bank charges (very modest) with the publisher, but whether or not to bear half the cost of the publisher's sub-agent's 10 percent commission should depend on the negotiated split in foreign rights. In practical terms, if the license for rights in Italy, for example, calls for a $2000 advance, and the author publisher split is 80/20, the publisher's net is approximately $1800 (after the sub-agent's 10 percent commission), of which the writer receives $1440. If the writer's split calls for less than 80 percent, I recommend deleting "agent's commission" from this clause (in some contracts this would be accomplished by changing the author's share from "net receipts" to "gross receipts").

Incidentally, a few contracts still contain a provision, in this or in some other clause, stipulating that if the royalty and rights revenue due for a particular period or year exceeds a certain amount (it can range from $2500 to $10,000), the publisher retains any moneys in excess of that amount—on the writer's behalf—until the following or subsequent periods, when the total amount due is less than the stipulated cutoff figure. Presumably, the purpose of this provision is to protect the author from high taxes resulting from a windfall, such as might come from an impressive paperback rights sale. A writer should delete this "shelter," since there are other ways to reduce taxes, such as income averaging. The rewards of this provision seem one-sided to me, permitting the publisher to earn 10 percent interest on the writer's $25,000 (or whatever), with no clear benefit to the writer.

> 20. In the event of the bankruptcy, insolvency or liquidation of the Publisher, this Agreement shall terminate and all rights granted to the Publisher herein shall revert to the Author automatically and withouc the necessity of any demand or notification.

20. Publisher's Bankruptcy, Insolvency, or Liquidation. This clause, if not found in the writer's contract, should be inserted as a rider. Once Chapter 11 bankruptcy or some other financial disaster strikes a publisher, control over the firm and its assets is turned over to the courts, and for all intents and purposes the author's property is frozen for months or even years. A better way to phrase it, and to cover some other contingencies, is as follows: "If the publisher shall default in the delivery of the advance, or semi-annual royalty statements and payments, and fail to deliver them after thirty (30) days' written notice, the agreement will terminate without further procedure and without prejudice to the author's claim for moneys due."

Many houses will accept this, and in the event that the publisher experiences "cash flow problems," which is occurring with increasing frequency at smaller houses, the writer will have sufficient influence to ensure that moneys due from his or her work will be a priority debt for the publisher (provided such a letter is sent as soon as a breach takes place). But if, in fact, your publisher goes bankrupt, this provision will not override the court's decision about what happens to the publisher's assets, one of which is your book. As this contract was issued by a major, very solvent house, I—perhaps carelessly—failed to make this insertion.

An additional provision well worth tacking on to this suggested clause might be: "Any dispute arising from this provision shall be settled through arbitration under the auspices of the American Arbitration Association." Any publishing dispute that has to be settled in a court of law will generally require exorbitant legal costs and stretch out for years. Since most writers can ill afford this, even were they certain of a favorable outcome, their inclination would be to settle out of court (for much less satisfaction, probably, than they felt was due them). However, arbitration proceedings, which are as binding as court proceedings, are much quicker and must less costly. Many publishers will accept this provision.

21. This Agreement shall be binding upon and inure to the benefit of the heirs, executors, administrators and assigns of the Author and the successors and assigns of the Publisher. Neither party hereto may make any assignment of this Agreement without the prior written approval of the other, provided, however, that the sale of substantially all of the assets of the Publisher, or its acquisition by or merger into another company, shall not be deemed an assignment of this Agreement by the Publisher.

21. Sale of Publisher's Assets. This clause permits the publisher to sell the firm's "assets" (which primarily consist of books both under contract and already published) without having to seek the writer's approval, provided the sale is of "substantially all of the assets of the Publisher. . . ." As these clauses go, this one is fair, since it permits an assignment without written consent only when "substantially all of the assets . . ." and so on. However, many contracts do not contain this qualification, in which case a writer should try to have it inserted.

By law, if publisher A acquires publisher B, publisher A is required to fulfill publisher B's contractual obligations. Of course, if the writer's editor is not one of the assets acquired by A, and if A is not as enthusiastic about the writer's book as B was, then the book is an orphan, and its fate may be preordained.

Note that—as is implied in this contract—without written consent, B cannot sell to A a writer's book if it is merely part of a series or imprint that B is selling. However, even though most contracts fail to include the phrase "without written consent," the publisher who uses this boilerplate clause and its very common wording does not in fact have the legal right to sell a writer's book without such consent. The purpose of including the phrase is to put a flag on it, so to speak, so as to spare the writer a potential legal hassle.

Another insertion some writers would wish to make, which no publisher would resist, and is found in many contracts, is a phrase that would appear right after "Neither party hereto may make any assignment of this agreement . . .," stating, "except for moneys due the author." This qualification permits a writer to assign moneys due to heirs, creditors, or a corporation later formed by the writer after publication, or to whomever, without requiring the publisher's consent. But it would be hard to think of a case in which the publisher would deny such consent.

22. This Agreement contains the entire understanding of the Author and the Publisher with reference to the Work; there are no representations, convenants or warranties other than those expressly set forth herein. No waiver or modification of any of the terms hereof shall be valid unless in writing and signed by both parties. No waiver of any breach shall be deemed a waiver of any subsequent breach.

23. Regardless of the place of its physical execution, this Agreement is being made under, and shall be governed by the laws of the State of New York.

24. The caption headings in the margins of this Agreement are inserted for convenience only and are without substantive effect.

25. This Agreement shall be of no force and effect unless signed by both parties within 60 days of the date first above written.

26. Agency Clause: All sums of money shall be paid to the Author's agent, The Balkin Agency, 850 W. 176 Street, New York, NY 10033, and receipt of said agent shall be a valid discharge of such indebtedness, and said agent is hereby empowered by Author to act on his or her behalf on all matters arising from and pertaining to the Agreement. For services rendered and to be rendered, Author does hereby irrevocably assign to said agent a sum equal to 10% (20% on British) of all gross monies accruing to the Author with respect to this Work.

IN WITNESS WHEREOF, the parties have signed this Agreement on the date first mentioned above.

_____
Author

_____
Editorial Director

AUTHOR'S SOCIAL SECURITY NUMBER _____
AUTHOR'S CITIZENSHIP _____
AUTHOR'S BIRTH DATE _____
(This information is needed for copyright purposes.)

22. Completeness of Contract. This clause does not mean that riders are not an express part of the contract, but primarily that to validate subsequent changes—such as an extension of the delivery date—they should be in writing and agreed to by both parties. The last sentence means that if the publisher agrees to any breach of the contract, whether amended in writing or not—for example, by accepting a manuscript 50 percent longer than is stipulated in the contract, or by agreeing to secure the artwork or permissions—this "waiver" does not invalidate any other of the author's obligations, or the contract itself.

23. Jurisdiction. Virtually all houses require that the contract be governed by (and in most instances disputed in) the state in which the house is located. This makes it a lot more costly and hectic for a writer living out of that state to contest the contract, should such a necessity arise, but all publishers would resist a change of applicable law to the writer's home state for reasons legal, logistical, or both.

24. Caption Headings.   Only a lawyer could make an improbable but persuasive argument for including this clause in a contract.

25. Signatures of Parties.   This clause prevents an unsigned contract from remaining indefinitely in limbo; it is reasonable for any publisher to set such a time limit.

26. Riders to Contract.   Here is where agreed-upon riders are inserted, which in this contract consists of a common agency clause.

The reason some agencies do not insist on a separate "Author/ Agent Agreement" is that the agent is protected by this clause, especially in that all moneys come directly to the agency. If an agent is employed to negotiate a contract, the writer is better off, for a variety of reasons, negotiating and signing a separate author/agent agreement, although an agency clause may still be inserted as a rider into the contract. For an exploration of this issue, see the Recommended Reading list for several citations of books that discuss author/agent relations in some detail.

Additional Riders or Provisions.   During the course of our discussion in this chapter, the insertion of a number of possible riders or provisions has been suggested. We might propose an almost indefinite number of others to cover an indefinite number of possible scenarios—for instance, a rider that provides additional advance money or a change in the share of certain rights if a book appears on the best-seller list, further qualified by the number of weeks it appears on the list—but it might lead us down an endless path.

On the other hand, a work of nonfiction may for one reason or another suggest to the author certain clauses, provisions, riders, changes, or deletions that are fair and particularly pertinent. For instance, an artist whose works are being illustrated in an expensive coffee-table format might want to insist on the right to closely examine and approve the color reproduction proofs before the book is printed. Each writer will have to decide for him- or herself whether some issue is both relevant and crucial enough to be negotiated for the contract.

But it is important to remember that oral assurances do not represent legally binding commitments, and that any significant issue should be settled in writing; sometimes an editor or a house will agree to make a commitment in a letter but not to incorporate it in the contract. Examples of these might be: to send the author on a promotional tour, to provide a certain sum for an advertising budget, to submit a certain number of bound galleys for blurbs or to a minimum number of bookclubs, and so forth. Although such a letter is not as airtight as a contractual provision, it still offers far more protection than an oral assurance and is an alternative to bear in mind.

It should be clear by now that most contracts and many clauses *are* negotiable, and writers should not be daunted by a protracted negotiation, since an ounce of prevention. . . . All contracts favor the publisher, and it is suitable, fair, and common to try to equalize the imbalance.

3

Contracts of specialized book publishers

Trade books are but one segment of the book publishing industry. Of the dozen or so other categories, several—such as Bible, encyclopedia, or subscription (of the Time-Life variety)—are of very specialized interest and are therefore omitted from our discussion. But a number of others are more commonly encountered. These divisions include mass market books, juvenile books, religious books, textbooks—whether elementary, high school, or college—professional books, and those of university, regional, and small presses. These other houses or divisions issue contracts that are remarkably similar to one another and to those for trade books, although they are almost always briefer. The basic components are virtually the same: clauses that spell out the territory, the author's warranty and indemnity, the royalties, the next-book option, and so forth. In most cases, subsidiary rights play a smaller role and are less likely to be exercised or sold. As a consequence, many of these contracts lump them together and offer the writer a 50/50 share. This should be resisted; as with trade book contracts, a number of rights are conventionally negotiable.

The reason these contracts are generally shorter is that they do not spell out as many contingencies as trade book contracts, nor do they detail a number of the components or responsibilities of the author/publisher relationship. It may be that because litigation is less common in most of these other divisions, the publishers have not felt the need to protect themselves with as much small print.

The major ways in which the contracts differ are in their ground rules: that is, in what is conventional industry-wide practice, and in what variations there are in policy from house to house. For example, 99 percent of textbook publishers pay royalties based on *net* receipts. But whether they commonly offer a 10 percent, 12½ percent, or 15 percent royalty or escalate from 10 to 15 or even 18 percent is a matter of negotiation and individual house policy. What *is* common to all these divisions is that their contracts are negotiable, although the following reservations are worth noting.

Mass market houses aside, these divisions are more modest in the amount of advance money they are willing to spend—with some exceptions for best-selling authors—and tend to be less flexible in their willingness to negotiate a number of clauses and provisions that are normally negotiable at trade book houses. In part, this is due to the fact that most agents do not swim in these waters (this is obviously not true of mass market and juvenile houses), and it is primarily as a result of the rise of the agent in the post-war years, that flexibility in publishing negotiations has come to be accepted. As a consequence, many editors are not as accustomed to negotiating, not as familiar with the meaning or ramifications of clauses in their own firm's contract, and sometimes taken aback by a knowledgeable author's requests. This may require an extra measure of both firmness and diplomacy. (For a fascinating description of the way it once was, readers will find George Gissing's novel *New Grub Street* (available in paperback from Penguin Books) an eye-opening and depressing depiction of the life and finances of Victorian writers.)

Let me digress for a moment to point out that religious book houses, which are often thought of as a separate category of publishing, are, for all intents and purposes, no different from trade book houses—when it comes to contracts and negotiations—except that their advances tend to be lower and their contracts somewhat less detailed. In all other respects, writers will find the discussion and suggestions for trade books applicable. This is equally true for regional presses, which differ from trade houses mainly in that they put out books that have more regional than national appeal (and hence smaller first printings and lower sales expectations) and perform all other publishing tasks on a smaller scale.

In discussing contracts and negotiations with these other divisions, I will confine myself to the most salient elements that reflect industry-wide practice, examine the areas of royalties and advances, and touch on those contractual factors that are particularly germane to each category of publisher. As with trade book contracts, those authors who have an impressive track record or a national reputation will have more leverage in their negotiations and should be able to command higher advances and royalties, a better share of rights, and a contract generally more favorable to writers than is conventional.

MASS MARKET BOOKS

Most "rack size" books, those that fit into the metal racks in bookstores, drugstores, supermarkets, or airline terminals, measure 4¼" by 7", and most of us tend to think that it is their size that distinguishes them from the larger trade paperbacks (where there is little uniformity of trim size). In fact, the primary distinction is in the distribution channels. Trade paperbacks (and hardcovers) are sold directly to bookstores by publishers' reps; mass market ("MM" hereafter) books are also sold to bookstores by reps, but more than half of the books are sold to nonbookstore outlets by a middleman, the "I.D." (independent dealer) or "Rack Jobber," who often both sells and chooses which titles will be carried by which outlets. The type of store, the location, and the demographics determine the I.D.'s distribution patterns for genres and individual titles.

Minimum first year's sales estimates of 35,000 copies and upward are the ruling factor here in the decision about whether to publish and how much advance to pay for a book that is often here today and gone tomorrow. The rack life of an MM book can be as short as six weeks and is rarely longer than six months (excluding the small percentage of back-list classics of both literary fiction and genre novels, as well as best-selling and backlist nonfiction). Sometimes a title is shipped to outlets in cartons that are never opened but are returned to the I.D. or publisher a month to six weeks later; there just wasn't any rack space left for these mid-list titles. An equally dismaying corollary is the MM book signed up to fill a slot; that is, a major house (of which there are now eight) is expected by the I.D.s to ship, say, twenty-four titles a month. If the production schedule in March shows an unfilled slot for July, there will materialize a quickie, whose publishing fate is to go out on a wing and a prayer. In fact, this is the fate of most of the roughly 4000 MM books published every year. A certain number of potential best-selling titles are designated "leads," (about 10 to 15 percent) and a certain number, by virtue of the author's track record or the particular genre (such as a historical romance), are likely to sell in predictably high numbers. But as for the rest. . . . Most of the eight major houses issue roughly twenty to thirty titles a month, although Bantam, the leader, issues close to sixty.

In general, the minimum quantity for a first printing of a new title is 50,000 copies, even though—unlike statistics for all the other divisions in book publishing—the publisher may earn a profit on sales as low as 20,000 copies (contrast this with the minimum hardcover first printing of 5000 copies and about 10,000 to 15,000 copies for trade paperbacks). The reason for this is twofold: Because returns average 40 to 45 percent, roughly twice as high as those for hardcovers or trade paperbacks, the publisher has to ship 50,000 copies in order to expect to be able to sell 25,000 or more. Secondly, because first printings are so high, the unit costs are low; in fact, the unit cost may represent no more than one-tenth of the list price— half as much as for other publishing formats. It follows that the size of the first printing will not bear as much of a relationship to the amount of the advance as it will for other books. Books that are being reissued, redistributed, or reprinted—as well as titles that sell primarily to regular bookstores, such as classics—may be printed in quantities as low as 25,000.

In recent years, no more than half of the MM books published have been reprints of hardcovers, whereas up until about 1975 roughly two-thirds to three-quarters of them were, and advances from multiple submissions or auctions conducted by the hardcover houses frequently brought in revenues of six figures. But no longer. Fewer hardcovers are sold for MM reprints rights, and fewer dollars are paid up front for them (both of which factors account for the rise in numbers of trade paperbacks issued by the originating hardcover publishers). Reprint offers for $2500 to $3000 are common for books that ten years ago would have commanded double that amount.

Another recent phenomenon that writers may encounter is the "hard-soft deal." Nowadays, all MM houses but one (Avon

Books) have hardcover divisions and imprints. Agents as well as writers are now more frequently conducting auctions or making submissions to MM houses with the understanding that the publisher will issue the book first in hardcover and then, normally a year later, in an MM paperback edition (or even in a trade paperback format, since virtually all these houses have such imprints too; moreover, the decision about format may be withheld until the house sees what kind of reception the hardcover has had). The advantage to a writer of a hard-soft deal is that instead of sharing the MM royalties with the originating hardcover publisher, he or she gets to keep 100 percent. The disadvantage is that since no paperback auction is conducted, there is no chance of getting and sharing a large advance from the auction—of $100,000 or even higher (bear in mind that much less is much more common). Writers of hardcover books with MM potential, such as a hefty historical novel, will want to bear these options in mind when deciding where to submit their books.

Advances, save for those few books with clear best-selling potential, or by writers with impressive track records, are generally lower than for hardcover trade books. Genre novels—such as science fiction, mysteries, romances, international intrigue, or male adventure—generally command advances in the $3000 to $10,000 range; nonfiction is a bit lower. A writer's first book will command an advance at the lower end. Generally, MM houses like to develop genre writers who can be counted on to turn out two to five titles a year. These writers are given higher advances after the first book or two.

Conventional MM royalties for originals begin at 6 percent for the first 150,000; 8 percent thereafter. Writers will definitely want to resist lower royalties and should try to improve this standard by asking for 8 percent escalating to 10 percent after anywhere from 150,000 to 300,000 copies. In all other aspects, MM contracts are virtually identical to those for trade hardcover books, although writers will want to note the following few differences.

A sub-rights provision in the MM contract will permit the publisher to license the hardcover rights. A few books that may have a modest potential sale for simultaneous publication in hardcover—for example, a dictionary of sex slang—are not appropriate hardcovers for the MM house. This is primarily because such publishers limit their output of hardcover books to those that have the potential to sell 10,000 or more copies and fully intend to wait up to a year or more before issuing the paperback. The standard split for this right is 50/50, whereas 75/25 or 80/20 is fair and commonly accepted, with the added provision that the publisher "pass through" the author's share of the advance within thirty to sixty days of receipt *before* the originating publisher's advance is earned out.

The reserve-against-returns policy is a controversial one here, because some publishers will withhold as much as 65 to 75 percent of royalties due, as a reserve. Indeed, the reserve may not even be listed on the statement; the publisher may report only 25 to 50 percent of the sales (which actually means 25 to 50 percent of books shipped, but not yet paid for). MM houses routinely resist any restrictions on their reserve policies, but writers should nontheless attempt to obtain them, both in the percentage—35 to 50 percent—withheld and in the number of periods—two to four (that is, one to two years).

All other rights provisions, as well as most other clauses, would be negotiated in the same way as for trade book contracts.

CHILDREN'S BOOKS

Children's books, generally known in the trade as "juveniles" and "young adults" (from about ages eleven to sixteen), are normally published by divisions of trade book houses. In the past few years many changes have taken place in both editorial and marketing policy, in large part because libraries, which traditionally represented more than 80 percent of book sales, now constitute no more than half the market. One result is more paperback originals, fewer hardcovers, an increase of sales through juvenile book clubs, and an explosion of interest and sales in paperback teenage romances (and somewhat less so in adventure, horror, and novelty books). Most of these titles are developed in series. As well, the line between young adult and adult fiction has become fuzzier, to the extent that some books are marketed to both audiences. Even some traditional juveniles have broken out and become bestsellers as a result of the adult readership. Two examples are Shel Silverstein's *A Light in the Attic* (1983), and, more recently, *The Butter Battle Book* (1984), by Dr. Seuss.

One key difference between juvenile and trade books is that books for younger children, up to about the age of eight, are normally illustrated. Where these illustrations represent a significant feature or portion of the book, the publisher will generally choose the illustrator, who commonly receives half the advance and royalties, although in some cases, of course, the writer is also the illustrator. Writers will want to try to secure approval or at least consultation regarding the choice of an illustrator. Well-known illustrators working with writers of first books may command a 60/40 split.

Contracts and negotiations are virtually identical to those for trade books, except that advances tend to be more modest, and royalty escalations, especially for hardcovers, tend to start at higher numbers. Advances for juveniles range from $3000 to $6000; writers with impressive track records, of course, may command higher figures. The common royalty rate is 10 percent to 10,000 copies, 12½ percent thereafter. However, many contracts escalate to 15 percent after the sale of 20,000 to 25,000 copies, and this should be requested. Because of rising production costs, especially of color illustrations, some publishers begin with lower royalties for the first printing, which is usually about 10,000 copies. Some full-color picture books are so expensive to produce that publishers have a first printing of at least 15,000 copies and will not escalate royalties beyond 10 percent.

Library editions are often set apart in contracts, with royalties paid on *net receipts* rather than on list price. This is a provision writers should try to delete, since this means half of all sales. One conventional trade book provision is more crucial for juveniles: namely, the reduction on royalties for reduced printings. Because juveniles typically are backlist books (selling over a period of years), writers will want to resist the common reduction of "50 percent of prevailing royalties for sales made from reprinting of 2500 copies or less." Try to change this to three-quarters or two-thirds of prevailing royalties from printings of 1500 or fewer copies (or when semi-annual sales do not exceed 500 copies).

Young adult (YA) book royalties are often the same as for trade books, and writers should try to negotiate the standard 10 percent to 5000 copies, 12½ percent to 10,000, and 15 percent thereafter for hardcovers; and for trade paperbacks, 7½ percent to 20,000 copies, 10 percent thereafter. Most YA paperbacks are now being published as MM originals, and the royalties are generally the same as those that are most common for adult MM—that is, 6 percent to 150,000, 8 percent thereafter. While royalties lower than that should be resisted, authors might try to start out with a flat 8 percent or request a three-tiered escalation, going up to 10 percent after the sale of 300,000 copies. Don't be daunted by these numbers: The first twelve titles of Bantam's "Sweet Valley High" series of teenage romances have sold 5.2 million copies as of this writing.

More than half of the current crop of these teenage romances (and several other genres, such as horror, adventure, and mystery) are written for series, many of which are developed by "packagers." Packagers are middlemen who generally contract with publishers for individual books or series, based on outlines, and then find and contract with writers to complete the books. These contracts provide for an advance usually equal to those from publishers but then take 50 percent or more of the royalties. In some cases the writer is hired for a flat fee (signing a "work for hire" agreement), entitling him or her to no royalties or share of rights. Working with packagers has its advantages in that writers don't have to think up plots or solicit publishers for contracts, and packagers often supply steady employment. However, only apprentice writers will not resent the typical work-for-hire arrangement, for if a book is successful it seems only fair that the writer should share in the bounty, unless—as rarely happens—writers are more than handsomely paid for their time. Incidentally, packagers are an increasingly active source of supply for adult MM publishers, especially for romances, erotica, and male adventure novels.

One other provision to attend to is that which spells out commercial or merchandising rights, which are more likely candidates for exploitation with juveniles than with adult books. Original characters, such as Smurfs or those from "Sesame Street," may take on a life of their own, so to speak, and be licensed for use by manufacturers of dolls, calendars, stickers, toys, and whatnot. Moreover, other media spin-offs, particularly TV adaptations, can result from very successful books. Writers will therefore want to improve on the standard 50/50 split by trying to retain 100 percent or falling back to 90, 80, or 75 percent and retaining the right to approve any performance, commercial, or merchandising license.

Yet one more subdivision of children's books is MM originals for juveniles. These appear mostly in series, are not generally published in the conventional MM trim size, may have "paper over board" covers rather than standard MM paperback covers, and are "mass market" only in the sense that they have bigger first printings, which average 20,000 to 25,000 copies but can go as high as

50,000 to 75,000 for classics such as *Pat the Bunny* and *The Little Engine That Could*. Some leaders in the field are Random House, Western, and Grosset, which often have new titles written in house by staff, rather than buy them from free-lance writers. In this format and genre, publishers frequently pay writers flat fees in the $2500 to $5000 range, especially for books that are spin-offs from electronic media characters, such as from "Sesame Street," Walt Disney productions, and the Smurfs. Writers, of course, should resist this and try for at least a minimal share in potentially successful books. Royalty rates may begin as low as 4 percent, escalating to a high of 6 percent after the first printing, usually 20,000 to 25,000 copies.

Successful juveniles, unlike most trade books, often have a very long life as backlist titles, selling over a period of twenty or more years. In negotiating your contract, therefore, keep the long-term view in mind.

COLLEGE TEXTBOOKS

Advances for textbooks are common, but they sometimes bear little relationship to the anticipated first year's revenue. Since virtually all texts are written by professors, who are on salary, it is not uncommon for an editor to reply to a request for an advance, either politely or pugnaciously, by saying, "What do you need it for?"—implying that the sole purpose of advances is to finance living expenses. Rather than educate or argue, my advice is to answer this question on its own grounds, even if some deception is involved, by saying, for example, that you generally teach summer school, and writing the text means forgoing that necessary income (for two summers?), which has to be replaced; or, that you will *probably* have to take half a year off at half pay or no salary (either or both of which may in fact be true) to do justice to the book and complete it within a reasonable amount of time.

Regardless of the editor's point of view on advances, you can be sure that his or her firm *does* pay advances, and that the rule of thumb for trade books should guide the negotiation—that is, a writer should ask for approximately the amount of royalties the book would earn in its first year, based on the editor's estimate of sales. Incidentally, this rule of thumb applies to all these other divisions, save for small (alternative/independent) presses.

In practical terms, the writer who is proposing a book for a standard upper-level course, such as "Argumentation and Debate," a communications course, would ask the editor for an estimate of sales and the book's tentative list price (brook no hemming and hawing; editors *must* make these projections before they can make an offer). If the first year's sales estimate is 4000 copies, with a tentative list price of $17.95, then based on a 15 percent of net royalty—the most common hardcover text royalty—we can calculate a reasonable advance as follows. The textbook publisher's "net" is commonly 80 percent of the list price, since text publishers give bookstores an average 20 percent discount. (This is beginning to creep higher, to 25 to 30 percent, since college bookstores, which operate on an overhead of about 26 percent, are losing money selling texts.) Thus the publisher nets $14.36 on each copy. The royalty—15 percent—is therefore $2.15 per copy, which, when multiplied by 4000, works out to $8600. However, since textbook publishers also have "returns," we will deduct 20 percent from that figure, leaving us with $6880, which we will round off to $7000. To get this $7000, it is better to start off by asking for at least $8000. Any offer of less than $5000 for this book is patently unfair.

Introductory texts—for freshman and sophomore courses with large enrollments—are the fast lane in text publishing and are both riskier and potentially more remunerative for publishers, but the same rule of thumb should apply. A text for "Social Problems," a standard sophomore course in sociology, may have a potential annual nationwide market of 250,000, broken down into two or three levels (A schools, B schools, and junior and community colleges). A savvy, experienced editor who knows where the gap for a good text is, what is missing from the competing books there, and how to develop the ideal book for that level is capable of making a much more accurate estimate of potential sales than his counterpart in trade book publishing. If the first year's sales estimate is 15,000 copies, then an advance of $25,000—using the same formula as in the preceding paragraph—is not out of line. However, editors calculating advances for introductory texts will also factor in the author's reputation as well as his or her previous book's sales, which may result in a lower or higher offer.

The royalty rates in textbook publishing range from a low of 10 percent of net to a high of 20 percent. The most common royalty for a hardcover text is 15 percent, and for a paperback, 12½ percent. Escalations are less common than for trade book contracts but are fair and should be requested. The most sensible formula is to escalate at the second printing; that is, if the first printing is 7500 copies, the royalty escalates from 12½ to 15 percent after 7500 copies. Fifteen percent is about as much as textbook publishers will give for a paperback that is priced below approximately $15, but if the rate begins at 10 percent, then a two-tiered escalation to 15 percent is reasonable. With hardcovers, some publishers are resistant to going above 15 percent, but since production (plant) costs are assimilated in the first printing, profits are higher in the second and successive printings, and an escalation is fair *if* the second and successive printings exceed 5000 copies (the publisher's unit cost for printings up to 5000 copies may be too high to warrant paying a higher royalty). Thus, one might suggest an escalation to 17½ or 18 percent if the second printing exceeds, say, 6000 copies, or, more commonly, in any given year when sales exceed 10,000 to 15,000 copies (in which case printings would always exceed 6000 copies). An escalation to 20 percent is sometimes given for introductory texts, when printings or sales in any given year exceed 25,000 to 50,000 copies.

"Readers"—that is, anthologies—are much more common in textbook than in trade book publishing, and the foregoing guidelines hold true here except for the need to calculate and negotiate the permissions fees and budget. Generally, the editor will establish a permissions budget, which will be charged to the author's future royalty account and paid by the publisher upon publication. (Both parties recognize that it is an estimate, and should the writer exceed it by no more than 15 to 20 percent, most houses will go along with that. Above that, writers will probably be asked to delete or make substitute selections.) The editor will justifiably reduce the size of the advance against royalties. Some houses—especially when the author has a national reputation or an excellent track record—will agree to absorb half of or even all the permissions costs and will also agree to do the paperwork necessary to secure permissions. The latter is such a headache that I urge all writers to try to negotiate for it, even in exchange for a slightly smaller advance.

There are usually no potential rights sales for textbooks, and publishers generally offer an across-the-board 50/50 split. Fewer than one out of one hundred books will "travel"; that is, can be marketed in the British Commonwealth (and virtually never in translation to foreign countries). In those few instances where an author feels that there is some possibility—for example, a computer-language textbook—he or she should hold out for a 75/25 split.

Textbook publishers will occasionally agree to pay a "grant-in-aid," a nonreturnable sum, ranging from $500 to $2500, to cover the cost of a final typing or unusual expenses, such as hiring a research assistant, computer time, travel, preparation and solicitation of questionnaires, cost of securing camera-ready charts or tables from a statistician, and so forth. A separate provision will merely state: "Publisher agrees to provide a grant-in-aid of $XXX payable upon receipt of an acceptable manuscript." Incidentally, it goes without saying that should the author be responsible for delivering camera-ready artwork, and if it is a significant feature of the book, such as for a text on biology, writers must estimate and negotiate for a separate budget (the amount of which will normally be charged to the author's royalty account). Or, ideally, you may be able to persuade the editor to secure the artwork, based on your list or suggestions. In textbook publishing it is more customary than in trade book publishing for the publisher to supply the artwork.

An important clause to negotiate regards revisions. A few texts go into multiple editions (such as Samuelson's *Economics*, now in its twelfth edition, McGraw-Hill, 1985). The revision clause, as normally written, may be unfair on several accounts. Authors should clearly have the first opportunity to prepare the revision, as well as the right to choose or to "approve" the publisher's choice of revisor if, for whatever reason, the author chooses not to prepare it. (Where "approval" is granted to either party, it is usually qualified by the phrase "which shall not be unreasonably withheld.") Secondly, the author should receive an additional "reasonable advance against royalties, to be mutually agreed on at the time this clause is invoked." Lastly, if the author fails to prepare the revision, the approved "revisor" of the first revision should receive no more than a 25 percent share of the royalties, and no more than a 50 percent share of all successive revisions.

One other bugaboo to be wary of is a provision that requires the author to prepare a study guide, instructor's manual, workbook, or sets of test questions. It's one thing to ask a writer to prepare a ten-page manual or a dozen tests, and quite another to expect the writer to provide, gratis, a 120-page workbook or study guide that is given away. Any request for more than modest instructional apparatus should be separately compensated, either for a reasonable flat fee or, if the supplementary materials are to be sold (e.g., a student workbook), for an additional advance against royalties. Ideally, these extras are farmed out by the editor to a freelancer at the publisher's expense (whose work the writer agrees to evaluate and edit at the publisher's request).

For some reason—no textbook editor has yet provided me with a sound reason—many text houses make a fuss about copyrighting the book in the publisher's rather than the author's name. This should be resisted, and here you may want to educate the editor by referring to the reasons given on page 67.

Most other clauses and provisions in college textbook contracts, whether major or minor, are virtually identical to those found in trade contracts.

ELEMENTARY AND HIGH SCHOOL TEXTS

The "el-hi" publishers, as they are known in the industry, are primarily found as divisions in houses that also publish college texts and trade books. Well over 50 percent of el-hi books are published by approximately two dozen large publishers, such as McGraw-Hill, Macmillan, and Prentice-Hall, although there are, in fact, close to one hundred such houses.

There are several main differences between el-hi and college text publishing. In general, el-hi editors, most of whom are former teachers, generate their own ideas for texts, and then go out and find appropriate authors. By "appropriate authors" I mean that most texts have three or four authors, and editors look for a geographical spread, often focusing on those twenty-nine or so states that make "blanket adoptions"; that is, those states in which a committee selects books that are then used statewide. Consequently, it can be difficult to sell a text here on your own. The stakes and profits in el-hi publishing are high. First printings are a minimum of 25,000 copies, and books have to sell 100,000 copies over a five-year period to be profitable. When they do, the net profit margins are more than 15 percent, twice that of trade books.

One would think, therefore, that el-hi publishers are generous with advances and royalties. T'ain't so. Advances here are usually token and rarely match or exceed $5000 per author. Royalties for elementary school texts range from 4 to 6 percent and can descend to as low as 1 to 2 percent for basal readers or math series (and still have to be divvied up among several authors!). Junior-high texts go up to 7 percent, and high school text royalties are in the 8 to 10 percent range. Escalations are not common in el-hi text publishing, but they should be requested—for example, 5 percent to 50,000 copies (for an elementary text), 6 percent thereafter; correspondingly for junior- and senior-high texts.

As with college texts, the revision clause is important here, but generally the writer's freedom of choice, approval, or consultation of the revisor is restricted. It is important to have approval or at least consultation of any revisor chosen by the publisher, and to restrict his or her share of the royalty revenue as much as possible. In general, el-hi publishers are resistant to negotiation, more so than college text publishers, since they have had virtually no experience with literary agents. Even so, reasonable arguments can be made for reasonable requests, and writers should not fail to take strong positions on crucial issues. Because the stakes are so high, the author who has been approached by an el-hi editor has already been screened, so to speak, and therefore has some leverage. In other respects, the el-hi contract is very similar to the college text contract.

PROFESSIONAL AND REFERENCE BOOKS

The broad umbrella of "professional and reference books" includes works in diverse fields, whether scientific, technical, legal, medical, academic, or otherwise. In essence, any work that is specifically written for and marketed to professionals generally falls under this rubric. Many of these publishers are divisions of large houses, such as McGraw-Hill and Prentice-Hall, whereas others are smaller houses devoted to one or more specialties.

From the publisher's point of view, the primary distinction between a trade book and a professional book is the discount offered to wholesalers and retailers, which ranges from 25 percent to 33⅓ percent off the list price. The consequence of this discount—trade book discounts range from 40 percent to 50 percent—is that most retail bookstores, such as the Dalton and Waldenbook chains, will not stock these titles. They are generally carried by college and university bookstores, as well as some specialty bookstores. The bulk of the sales are made by mail order and to libraries.

Most of these books have a high price tag, $20 and up, because the print runs are generally smaller and the books generally heftier, but also because most readers of professional books feel that they have to own them—perhaps because they are normally tax deductible—so the publishers can sell them at whatever price the traffic will bear.

While the contracts are quite similar to those for trade books—though usually briefer—there are some essential differences in industry-wide practice, and some provisions that are more crucial for writers. Advances are more modest than for trade books, ranging generally from $2500 to $10,000, although more and less are not uncommon. Royalties are almost always based on *net receipts*, ranging from 10 percent to 18 percent, with conventional escalations possible within this range. The most common royalty, however, is a straight 15 percent of net receipts.

Our trade and textbook rule of thumb—an advance based on estimated first year's sales and royalties—doesn't generally hold true here, since it would often mean a much higher advance than publishers are willing to pay. A 200,000-word *Geolinguistic Handbook* with an estimated price tag of $39.95 and an estimated first year's sale of 4000 copies translates into a royalty of roughly $4 per copy, which in a trade book house might garner an advance of $12,500 to $15,000 but is more likely in the professional book division to result in an offer of $5000 to $7500. This is not to suggest that writers shouldn't try to negotiate a large advance but only to explain that it is not common and conventional.

Two provisions worth paying special attention to are the ones that reduce royalties for export sales and for sales made from low print runs. Export sales—to Canada, the British Commonwealth, and around the world—sometimes constitute as much as one-quarter to one-third of total sales, primarily because many professional books are not translated but are read in the language in which they are published. Writers will want to try to improve on the conventional "50 percent of standard royalties" or "export royalties based on net receipts" (where discounts can run as high as 55 to 60 percent) by asking for three-quarters to two-thirds of standard royalties, or adding a provision such as "but in no case shall the royalty be less than [say, anywhere from 5 percent to] 10 percent of the U.S. list price." Negotiating a reasonable improvement over the standard reduction often requires some discussion with the editor regarding the house's prevailing export royalties, into which writers should not hesitate to inquire.

Many professional books are solid backlist titles that sell over a period of years, often going into second and successive editions. Frequently, the reprintings are low, ranging from 1000 to 2000 copies, so that writers will want to resist reductions in royalties for small printings of any quantity. The high list price gives the publisher a handsome profit; even if the unit price in a small reprinting is relatively costly, the house can still well afford to pay normal royalties.

Subsidiary rights are infrequently sold, except for book-club rights. More than one hundred small to medium-size book clubs sell professional books, and these sales are sometimes greater than bookstore and mail-order sales combined. The common book-club royalty is 10 percent of the offering price, of which the author normally gets 50 percent. Writers with some leverage may try to improve this split to 55/45 or 60/40 and to have the publisher "pass through" book-club revenue within thirty to forty-five days of receipt, rather than deducting it from the "unearned advance" and paying it out at semi-annual or annual royalty time, as is common.

A grant-in-aid, as with college texts, is sometimes given for a research assistant, final typing (or transferring to computer disks), or whatever; where one is appropriate, a writer should attempt to negotiate it. Since mail-order sales constitute such an important marketing channel, often representing one-quarter to one-third of total sales, writers may want to secure a provision in which the publisher guarantees a mailing piece that will go out to a minimum of X thousands of potential readers. (Incidentally, some professional-book publishers, if pressed, will increase the standard 5 percent mail-order royalty to 7½ percent.) By supplying the editor with specific membership data for the appropriate organizations, clubs, newsletters, journals, and so forth, the writer will be in a stronger position to negotiate such a flyer and/or perhaps ads in appropriate professional media. Most editors will assure writers that such promotional efforts are a *sine qua non* for marketing the book, but such commitments in writing will ensure the effort when the time comes. Since the time from proposal to publication may be as much as from two to five years for professional books, it is prudent to get all assurances for future performance written into the contract.

UNIVERSITY PRESSES

Over the past five years, many university presses have undergone major changes in both house policy and in image. Increasingly, they have begun to diversify and to publish more poetry, fiction, short story collections—for which the university presses of Pittsburgh, Illinois, and Missouri in particular have a reputation—serious nonfiction suitable for "general readers," and graduate-level textbooks. Some titles are even making the best-seller lists, such as . . . *And Ladies of the Club*, which was contracted by Ohio State University Press and then licensed to Putnam—an unusual arrangement. It would be stretching matters to say that these presses are going commercial, since the majority of the one hundred or so of them still traditionally publish monographs for academics and professionals and appropriate regional books (e.g., *The Missions of New Mexico Since 1776* and *Cajun Cooking*), but more than half a dozen of them now consistently publish books for readers outside of their traditional markets. The university presses of Chicago, Yale, Princeton, Indiana, Harvard, and California are the primary ones, whereas Cambridge's and particularly Oxford's university presses have for years published for a large spectrum of readers, and writers who negotiate with them should consider them as trade/text/professional publishers, depending on the individual title at hand. All eight of these houses will discount their general-reader books at standard trade publisher discounts in order to ensure sales through normal bookstore channels.

In most ways, university press contracts and negotiations are similar to those for professional books, especially with the larger and more ambitious ones, such as those eight listed here, which will commonly pay advances from $1000 to $5000 (sometimes, although rarely, going as high as the reputed $25,000 that Harvard and Oxford have on several occasions paid for desirable books). Most of the other presses limit their advances from $500 to a high of $2500, and it is common for there to be no advance at all.

Royalties are almost always based on net receipts and, unlike those for professional books, often start at 10 percent, escalating at 3000 copies to 12½ percent and going to 15 percent after the sale of 5000 copies (or some similar permutation). Incidentally, the median sale for a traditional university press hardcover is under 2000 copies. Paperback royalties may begin at 6 percent (of net) and escalate to

7½ or 10 percent after the sale of 5000 to 10,000 copies.

As with professional books, editors are less conversant with detailed negotiations, but that is no reason to avoid them. Even university press books have "break-out potential," especially those that are not clearly targeted for a small, professional, or academic audience. Whereas advances and royalties may be modest, and lower than for other divisions, writers should negotiate provisions that allow for the possibility that a book will be successful. Such provisions include approval of rights sales, retaining performance rights, and a "pass-through within thirty to sixty days" provision for revenue from rights sales where the author's share exceeds $500 (especially recommended, because most university presses send statements and pay royalties only once a year, instead of semi-annually).

SMALL PRESSES

Depending on which sources one quotes, there are anywhere from 2000 to 5000 small presses in the United States. By "small press" I do not mean that they are distinguished from other categories merely by the fewer number of books published per year, but rather that the kinds of books they publish, their marketing methods and channels, and their sales expectations and editorial interests and motives generally differ from those of trade book publishers. Variously referred to as independent, alternative or counter-culture publishers, these houses concentrate on experimental fiction, poetry, "new age" consciousness, offbeat or Oriental spiritual and religious topics, wholesome and natural means of feeding the mind or body, radical politics, and so forth. Some concentrate on deluxe limited editions of poetry and fiction, contemporary or classic, which are costly and more handsome and enduring than any books issued by trade houses, and some publish thirty-two-page chapbooks or pamphlets that are mimeographed and stapled. The range of quality, both in content and format, is enormous.

Profit is usually neither sought nor gained by most small presses, although a few of the old-timers, who manage to get more than modest national distribution and reputations (such as City Lights Books or Capra Press) by dint of grants and sales, sometimes make a small profit and sometimes work out distribution arrangements with trade houses. This pulls them into that gray area spanning small presses and trade books. And a few, such as Ten Speed Press, which has sold more than two million copies of *What Color is Your Parachute?*, are quite profitable and might more suitably be called "independent" rather than "small" or "alternative." Most, however, are strictly nonprofit, operate at a deficit, and subsist on very small budgets consisting of staff-member or patron support, grants, and modest sales revenues.

As a consequence, advances are rarely given, and authors are sometimes expected to help share the workload or expenses of production. Royalties are often conditional; that is, they are paid only after the sale of enough copies to cover the cost of production. Or, in lieu of royalties, authors are given 10 percent of the number of books on the first and future print runs. The third common royalty arrangement is the conventional 10 percent of list price or net receipts, escalating after the sale of 3000 copies to 12½ percent and perhaps to 15 percent after the sale of 5000 copies. Sometimes a combination of any two or three of these rates is offered.

Although few writers will negotiate their contracts here with profit in mind, it nevertheless pays to attend to the traditional contractual clauses and provisions, both because some of these houses are lax in doing so—which may leave writers open to future headaches—and because a few books that start out as small-press publications may eventually wind up at major trade houses, as did Joyce's *Ulysses*. Writers should therefore have approval over or at least be consulted about any rights sales or licenses and should retain first serial, performance, commercial, and even foreign rights (few small presses have the means or time to exploit these), as well as second serial rights, especially for poetry and short stories. Most small presses, incidentally, are more generous in the author/publisher split on rights—say, 90/10 or 80/20 for the sale of paperback reprint rights—or are more than willing to let the author retain many or all of them; authors should usually expect a better share than for trade books.

The sales of many small-press books result as much from the author's efforts as from the publisher's, often from poetry or fiction readings. Therefore, writers should ask for the right to purchase copies for a discount of 50 percent (with or without royalties paid). Although some of these presses issue boilerplate contracts (which are much briefer than those for trade book houses), some do not and will either send a casual letter of agreement to be signed by both parties or merely indicate in a letter the house's intention and policies. Authors should have more protection than these minimal missives afford and can either construct their own more detailed letter of agreement or avail themselves of a model small-press contract (with guidelines), written by the author of this book and published by Dustbooks, P.O. Box 99, Paradise, CA 95969 (available for $1 per copy).

Small presses are flourishing at the moment, and many works that would never see print at a trade house, either because the sales projections are estimated as too low or the subject matter is considered too offbeat, happily find themselves in print at small presses. Moreover, some small-press books become so successful, such as John Muir Publications' book on repairing the Volkswagen Beetle or *The Tassajara Bread Book*, that they catapult the publisher (who may be the author) into considerable success. If your book can't find a home in some other category of publishing house, don't write off the small press; many now-famous poets—for example, Pound, Lowell, Williams, and Rukeyser—had their first books published by small presses. Why not yours?

4

Creative negotiating

Now that we have reviewed the clauses and provisions of a typical trade book contract and made recommendations for changes, additions, and deletions, it will be useful to discuss a number of negotiating tips that some agents and some editors employ. Let us call them the tricks of the trade. There is nothing fancy or arcane about them—every person engaged in a business who either buys or sells something develops a kitful, whether through experience or training. Rather than think of employing these tactics to manipulate or defeat an opponent, as some do, or viewing the negotiating process as a David-and-Goliath confrontation, or girding yourself against someone's putting something over on you or taking advantage of you, remember that the book business—although not as genteel as some would imagine or like it to be—is still for most publishers a marginally profitable industry. Then, too, the editor you will negotiate with may neither be expert at it nor much more comfortable doing it than you are, and not nearly as interested in the "deal" as he or she is in the book.

It follows, then, that your approach should be low-key and diplomatic. After all, you are presumably more adept at wielding a pen than a sword and are certain to fare better by not taking an overly aggressive or defensive stance. This is not to say that you shouldn't be persistent or that you should capitulate on important points just because you don't want to make a big fuss or alienate your ally, the editor. Editors are quite accustomed to lengthy and sometimes exasperating negotiations, as well as to those that are short and sweet. In my experience, the attitude on both sides is: "When it's over, it's over."

Two elements of the negotiating process are so crucial that I hesitate to call them tips or tactics. The first is: *always take careful notes during any negotiation that takes place over the phone, and always reiterate at the end of the conversation any terms or provisions agreed on.* Just preface the recap by saying, "Let me make sure I have this right" and going over the points one by one. Most agents and editors make the mistake of forgetting to do this only once in their career. It doesn't hurt to write a confirming letter or to ask for one from your editor.

The second point is: *always check your notes against the contract itself.* When you have concluded your negotiations, some of the terms may be in a letter and some in notes you've taken during phone conversations. Always make doubly sure, when the contract arrives weeks later, that what you agreed on has, in fact, been incorporated into it. The editor will not personally have typed the contract, and mistakes are very easy to make, especially where numbers and small print are involved. When mistakes do appear in a contract, for some reason they always seem to be to the author's detriment! But this is not a publishing ploy, and there is no reason to panic. Just call your editor. In most instances, if you have been careful with *your* notes, he or she will routinely agree that it is a mistake, and ask you to change it, to initial the change(s) in the margin, and to send all copies back for counter-initialing.

TACTIC #1: BE PREPARED

Before you begin negotiating your contract, you should make a list of those elements that are crucial to you and on which you are unwilling to compromise. For many writers, the main issue may be the advance against royalties, especially if they are approaching the publisher with an outline and a sample chapter or two. Having carefully "guesstimated" that it will take you so much time to complete the book (invariably it will take you at least 25 percent longer than you imagine; now's the time to be realistic, not later), and that it will cost you so much for travel expenses or whatever, you will want to prepare a budget. It's for yourself—the editor isn't particularly interested in it. Ideally, it should cover your expenses and pay you a modest living wage during the course of writing the book. However, few authors, especially those with a first book, receive an advance sufficient to meet these criteria. This minimum figure, therefore, may or may not be your "fallback" position, the number below which you are not prepared to go. (Most writers earn their living at some more reliable trade and can afford to be more flexible, but virtually all expect and deserve an advance for the effort expended.)

Or perhaps your book will require a number of illustrations, and you anticipate that the cost of securing photos or line drawings is sufficient to warrant an "artwork budget" above and beyond the advance (the cost should exceed $500 if it is to warrant a separate budget). Or you feel it absolutely necessary that your book appear first in cloth, then a year later in paperback; or its ideal first format is as a trade paperback edition; or that the publisher has to be willing to sell your book to sporting goods stores in addition to normal book outlets. Depending on your book, and your unwillingness to accept less for what you feel are reasonable demands, you will establish one or more of these crucial sticking points, or "deal breakers," as they are sometimes called. These may also include royalty rates, publication date, retaining control or approval of certain rights, unusual expenses, how restrictive the option clause is, and so forth. Having a list, carefully arrived at, will prevent you from either committing yourself impulsively to something you will regret or rejecting something that turns out to be less than crucial.

You should also be prepared to answer any questions that are appropriate to your book, even if the information is contained in your proposal and sample. And by the way, your proposal should have contained all the possible ammunition available to strengthen your own credibility as a potentially successful writer, and to help your editor sell you and your book to the house: your credentials, your media experience (if any), the potential audience (supported by relevant statistics), the book's potential for special or premium sales, or any angle that might have a bearing on sales, and so forth. Editors sometimes forget, for example, that on page eight you provided a delivery date or the approximate length of your manuscript. Or he or she may ask questions raised by the marketing manager, editor-in-chief, or another editor present at the editorial meeting at which it was decided to make you an offer, provided that the house is satisfied with your answers to certain questions. The questions may concern the sales of your previous book(s), special organizations you have contacts with that might buy your book in quantity, your willingness to forgo color illustrations, names of scholars or noted professionals who might write a foreword to your book, or why you did not include X, Y, or Z. A different set of questions exists for every book; the more homework you have done and the more you can anticipate what might be asked, the better prepared you will be for a successful negotiation.

TACTIC #2: KNOW THE GROUND RULES

The ground rules in book publishing contracts consist of what is customarily negotiable at most trade houses (and how far you can go, so to speak) and what isn't, and what that particular house's "fixed policy" is regarding certain provisions. For example, most houses are flexible on trade paperback royalties, which can range from 5 percent of list to 10 percent of list; lower or higher than that is very unusual.

An example of a fixed policy that is common to most houses is the sharing of advances and royalties from book club sales with 50 percent to the publisher and 50 percent to the author. Of course, there are exceptions, but it is generally not fruitful to try to buck house policy or general industry practice. The problem is that house policy varies considerably from place to place—a few houses will pay only 10 percent of *net receipts* for a paperback royalty—and industry-wide custom is somewhat fluid and changeable. Clearly, it is a thorny problem to figure out what *your* publisher's fixed policies are, and how flexible the editor might be about other matters. Not only that, but contracts vary from two to twenty pages, and of the one hundred or so I have seen, none is exactly like another.

However, most book contracts, by and large, cover a fixed number of issues relating to the disposition of the rights to your work, other legal matters, your responsibilities, their responsibilities, and so forth. The depth of coverage may vary, the order may be different, the language clear or legalistic, and the number of possible contingencies spelled out modest or myriad. In our sample contract we have tried to show all the *major* provisions to be found in most contracts, and many of the minor ones. Industry-wide practice on most of these matters is fairly uniform; for example, trade hardcover book royalties are typically 10 percent of the list price for the first 5000 copies, 12½ percent for the next 5000 copies, and 15 percent thereafter. However, a number of houses do have a fixed policy of offering more modest rates—say, 10 percent for the first 10,000 copies. And, as mentioned earlier, a few trade houses pay royalties on "net receipts" rather than list price, or on net receipts on paperback only.

It follows, then, that you should not only carefully consider the information already provided in the discussion of what is or is not "generally" possible, but you also must feel out during the negotiation process what seems to be flexible and what appears to be inflexible. Here, common sense and the editor's reactions to certain demands are your best guides. If you are fortunate enough to know a writer who has a contract with that house, you can consult him or her; most of us aren't. The *Author's Guild Bulletin* annually publishes a summary of the results of several hundred authors' negotiations with trade houses. This is a very useful guideline but available to members only—a good reason for joining! Maybe you know or can get to know a member.

In most instances, however, you have to play it by ear, just as agents do. Of course, we have the advantage of past experience and the added resource of experienced colleagues to consult. One reason I recommend employing a literary lawyer over a general practice lawyer in Chapter 5 is that a number of customary practices may seem unreasonable or unfair to a local attorney, who may complicate your negotiations with "reasonable" requests that will not be accepted by 99 percent of the houses. The provision on "warranty and indemnity," for instance, strongly favors the publisher and often obligates the writer to bear the responsibility and high cost of defending against libel and invasion-of-privacy suits. (Fortunately, there is a trend toward extending the publisher's umbrella of libel insurance to writers. As of this writing, about two dozen major houses offer it, and more are likely to do so in the near future.)

In sum, the writer is playing a serious game that has its own set of rules, some of which are relatively fixed, others of which aren't. To be successful, to win the game, you must play within the framework already established. And don't expect to win 21 to 0.

TACTIC #3: AVOID THE TELEPHONE AS MUCH AS POSSIBLE

If you are more adept at writing than at talking on the telephone, resist an editor's suggestion, however insistent, to commit to final terms over the phone. "Terms" for most editors means an advance—"We are prepared to offer you X"—and royalties, usually proffered as "our standard royalties." You already know that negotiations and contracts involve quite a bit more than these elements, and financial issues are rarely "standard." If your initial conversation(s) includes an offer from the editor, it should not evoke more than an equivocal response from you, such as "I am delighted to have your offer, but I need time to think about it." Aside from the advance, you might want to go over your few "crucial" points on the phone. The editor may have to clear these with others. He or she may call back with counter-offers to your points, and this can go back and forth. Try to avoid firmly agreeing to counter-offers without sleeping on them. If you do reach an agreement, the editor will then be ready to have a contract drawn up and to send you a copy to scrutinize. At this point, you might request a blank boilerplate or "rough draft" of the contract in lieu of the "final" document (which is nonetheless just as negotiable as a draft). Some houses will agree to send it; others won't. A draft can be sent to a writer quickly; a final contract has to pass through various departments for approval and may take three to four weeks to arrive.

Make a photocopy, whether of the rough draft or the final contract, write or type in the additional changes you want on it, and return your photocopy with a covering letter that explains changes where necessary or appropriate. Your editor will then call you and conduct the final negotiation over the phone. You will either be asked to make the final changes, or to return the contract to be revised at the publisher's.

TACTIC #4: BE PATIENT

Patience is a virtue in contract negotiations, and sometimes it is as rare in agents as in writers. By the time a writer has a bona fide offer, he or she has probably spent months canvassing publishers, months (or years) writing the book, and many hours in fantasy of both the best and worst sort. Moreover, it is not uncommon for an "interested" publisher to take several months before coming to a decision. The weight of this burden of time takes its toll, and the mere mortal who finally gets the *offer* is sorely tempted to short-cut *any* further delays in the consummation. Furthermore, many writers, harboring the uncertainties about the merits of their work that most creative people do, worry that any hemming and hawing on their part may stimulate second thoughts on the other end. Or they wonder whether drawn-out negotiations or excessive demands will rock the boat and cause the editor to withdraw the offer.

An editor has yet to withdraw an offer from me, in more than a decade of agenting, because of protracted negotiations. Of course, there *are* limits to anyone's patience, and attempting to prolong a discussion of elements that are generally "non-negotiable" can prove counterproductive. But generally speaking, if you do not conduct the negotiation piecemeal, that is, by bringing up new points at successive stages—and I should stress that violating this precept is both irksome to editors and can be very counterproductive to a successful negotiation—and you remain reasonable and pleasant and use common sense and are prepared to compromise, it is not necessary to hurry things along.

TACTIC #5: EMPLOY UNORTHODOX PROVISIONS

You may make one or more contractual requests that you feel are important for *your* book but are not generally pertinent for most books or are not part and parcel of a standard contract. One not-so-uncommon provision guarantees that a flyer or brochure will be mailed to X, Y, or Z mailing lists, or to at least 20,000 members of your target audience. For example, a book on having your firstborn at the birth of your second should appeal to childbirth educators, pediatric nurses, and midwives, all of whom can most efficiently be reached by direct mail.

Promises of publicity, promotion, and advertising for your book that are not in writing often prove no more binding later on than declarations made after midnight in a dark corner at a fraternity-house party. Normal publishing procedure does not call for a flyer, but it is reasonable to request a provision for one if you have the kind of book and audience that warrant such an expense. However, provisions of this sort encompass a broad range of possibilities.

In negotiating my contract for this book, I was anxious to ensure that the publisher would, at some point, issue a paperback edition, since hardcovers usually have a very short shelf life (an average of three to six months). I felt that casual browsers in the reference or writing section of bookstores might well buy this book on impulse, so long as it remained in bookstores. After numerous phone calls back and forth, we agreed to insert a provision stating that when sales fall below eighty copies a month (around 1000 a year) or the inventory falls below 1000 copies, the publisher will issue a paperback, and *the author has the right to purchase inventory at cost plus 10 percent in order to reduce it to below 1000 copies.* In other words, if after two to three years the inventory is 1800 copies, I can buy 800 copies at roughly $2 per copy, if I feel it is then worth it to me to see a paperback edition. Since I think I can sell almost that many hardcover copies myself through inexpensive classified ads or a flyer (and make a handsome profit even if I offer a big discount), I probably will invoke that provision if it comes to that.

Here are a few brief examples of other provisions you might request:

- Increase the advance by suggesting that the publisher "pass through"—pay within thirty or forty-five days of receipt—your share of rights moneys (first serial, book club, British, or translation) rather than deduct it from your unearned advance, as is commonly done.

- Have the publisher agree to sell you books at a high discount (55 to 60 percent off list—40 percent is normal) if you buy in excess of, say, 250 copies. This is worthwhile if you think that, via lectures or through inexpensive ads or flyers, you can sell copies to a target audience or to specialty stores that the publisher will not canvass (your right to resell, and where, has to be incorporated into the contract).

- Agree to take out some coupon ads in specialty magazines that you cannot persuade the publisher to pay for but whose readership you feel will buy the book, with the provision that the publisher pay you a 10 percent royalty on all copies sold through the ad, rather than the conventional 5 percent. (It would be foolhardy to do this in *Playboy*, *Time*, or *People* magazines; it is usually economical only for carefully chosen specialty magazines whose readers are particularly interested in the topic of your book.)

You get the idea. Every nonfiction book has its own special twist— these unorthodox provisions rarely apply to fiction—and you will have to devise your own provision, if and when it is suitable.

TACTIC #6: REQUEST BONUSES; BARTER ADVANCES AND RIGHTS

Because most books represent a gamble whose odds disfavor the publisher by at least three to one, its primary concern is to minimize the financial risk. One obvious cost-cutting device is the author's advance, which is one of the more flexible portions of the "up front" money. It reasonably follows that in exchange for the author's accepting a lower advance than anticipated, the publisher should be correspondingly more generous when profits emerge—that is, when the publisher earns money beyond its break-even point. As well, the writer can trade off some shares of rights or royalties against others. Writers can capitalize on these principles during negotiation by requesting bonuses or by bartering both advances and rights. For example:

- Hardcover royalties escalate to 15 percent for the second printing (provided the first printing falls into the normal 5000 to 8000-copy range),thereby skipping the conventional 12½ percent interim escalation. A similar skip is equally suitable for trade paperback royalties.

- Escalate the author's normally fixed 50/50 share of paperback reprint rights to 55/45 after the first $25,000 or so, and then 60/40 after $50,000 or so.

- Increase the publisher's normal share of one right for another, such as giving the publisher 50 percent of first serial rights—in lieu of the common 90/10—in exchange for a larger advance or a greater share of paperback reprint or British rights.

- Request a $2500 to $7500 bonus for: each week a book appears on the *New York Book Review* or *Publishers Weekly* best-seller list (which can be broken down further by the book's position on the list, as well as the length of time it remains there).

- Request a bonus if a sale of film or TV mini-series rights is consummated, or for the appearance of a "movie tie-in" paperback edition. Ten percent of the "pick-up price" is where to start (the bonus could range from $10,000 for TV to $100,000 for a feature picture).

- Request a bonus if the book is chosen as a main or alternate selection by a major book club ($5000 to $10,000 would be reasonable).

- Agree to prepare the index yourself in exchange for an additional $500 advance (many nonfiction authors choose to have this prepared by the publisher's choice of a professional indexer).

Any number of permutations on this tactic may be conceived and accepted.

TACTIC #7: PLAY THE NUMBERS GAME

Throughout our discussion of contracts and agreements, whether for magazines, trade books, textbooks, or mass market books, dollar figures and royalty percentages naturally have played a key role. In most instances, the numbers are rounded off in the conventional publishing manner. That is, advances are cited as, say, $5000 to $10,000, or $3000 to $6000, and royalties—especially when escalations are discussed—have customary increments, such as 6 percent to 150,000 copies and 8 percent thereafter (for mass market royalties). Or, they may be 10 percent of net receipts for the first 3000 copies, 12 ½ percent for the next 3000 copies, and 15 percent thereafter (for college text paperbacks).

Most of us—agents and editors—who negotiate contracts have frequently fallen into a rut about these numbers, insofar as we rarely try to invoke the numbers we skip over, whether it is 11 or 13 percent; $8500, $21,000; or even 8 ½ percent or 9 ½ percent. Rounding off the numbers, whether dollars or royalties, is a habit that has turned into a custom. But it needn't govern *your* negotiation.

In negotiating an advance for a book or a fee for an article, it is common to have offers and counter-offers bandied back and forth. If a writer who is shooting for a $10,000 advance is at first offered $8000, most of us, including the two negotiators, are likely to assume that each party may settle on $9,000 as the compromise figure. Probably, but not always. Ten thousand dollars may invoke a mental stop sign for the editor-in-chief, but $9500 may not. Or maybe $9000 will, but $8500 will not. Where small amounts of money are concerned—say, the difference between a carton of milk at a convenience store for seventy-five cents and at the supermarket for sixty-five cents—most of us are inclined to buy our milk, most of the time, at the supermarket. Why throw out even ten cents? For some reason, however, when large sums are involved, we tend to be more cavalier, or automatically work things out in round numbers. But $500 is, you will agree, nothing to sneer at. Therefore, in negotiating for money with editors, who invariably think in round numbers, don't hesitate to try to squeeze out that extra $500 or even $250. It will buy a lot of cartons of milk.

Where royalty percentages are concerned, this strategy may ultimately earn (or lose) a writer thousands of dollars, *especially* if the book turns out to be successful. Take conventional mass market royalty rates: 6 percent to 150,000, 8 percent thereafter. Our discussion in the book suggested that the writer try to add another escalator: 8 percent to 300,000, 10 percent thereafter. Many houses will resist going over 8 percent (although 10, 12, or even 15 percent for authors with very impressive track records is common). The editor may reject your proposed escalation, but what if you counter with "What about 8 percent to 400,000, and 9 percent thereafter?" "Hmmm," she says. "I'll get back to you on that."

Let us surmise that the house agrees to it, as is at least a one-out-of-three possibility. Our putative book is priced at $2.95, so an 8 percent royalty means $.24 per copy, and 9 percent translates into $.27—a mere $.03-per-copy difference. Most mass market books do not sell more than 400,000 copies; indeed, most don't sell more than 100,000. But *if* yours is the one out of fifty that does, that sells, for example, 500,000 copies, you will have earned an extra $3000 in royalties. And what if it sells 750,000 copies, or a million?

Or perhaps you are placing a religious reference book with a professional book publisher—say, a 250,000-word *Handbook of Jewish Theology* slated to carry a $39.95 price tag. The editor offers to escalate your royalty from $12\frac{1}{2}$ percent of net receipts to 15 percent after the sale of 5000 copies but rejects an escalation to $17\frac{1}{2}$ percent after 10,000 copies. You counter with 16 percent after the sale of 7500 copies, and this is considered unorthodox but is accepted. For argument's sake, let us say that this book sells 4500 copies the first year, 3000 copies the second, and then 1750 copies for the next two years. The net price, with a typical 25 percent discount, is roughly $30, so the author will receive an extra $.30 per copy for the last two years' sales of 3500 copies, which works out to $1050. That too will buy a lot of cartons of milk.

Of course, one must draw a line somewhere; editors will certainly raise their eyebrows if a writer counter-offers a $1000 offer by asking for $1180, or asks for an escalation to $9\frac{1}{4}$ percent for our putative mass market book (but 1/2 percent escalations are *not* uncommon with paperbacks, whether mass market, trade, or otherwise). Many editors may be surprised by or resistant to these interim numbers, but only because "we've never encountered that before." Why not expand their horizons?

TACTIC #8: DON'T BE AFRAID TO ASK QUESTIONS

Those contracts whose language is perfectly clear are few in number. In most, the legalese ranges from difficult to tortuous. The justification for this is that ambiguities are avoided by the precision of legal minds, who have honed their words on the rock of truth. Obviously, those few contracts that can be read and understood by lay people disprove this "truism." There is no reason to feel embarrassed or to avoid showing your ignorance by failing to ask for a clear interpretation or explanation of the meaning of a phrase, provision, or clause that baffles you. You may be surprised to find that your editor is equally puzzled and has to "get back to you" about one or more of them. And you will occasionally find that the twisted phrase *is* ambiguous, and you will want it restated for purposes of clarity.

In addition, there are provisions whose ramifications are not apparent. These should be questioned. For example, many contracts contain a statement to the effect that when sales are made at a discount of 50 percent or more, royalties are reduced by half, paid on net receipts rather than list price, or reduced by a formula. The crucial point is what *percentage* of sales are made at a discount of 50 percent or higher (which in the first instance reduces your income by half). A few publishers sell half or more of their books at this discount, some sell a smaller percentage, and some include this provision in their contracts but almost never sell their books at a discount higher than 48 percent. Find out. If your publisher is one of those that sell upwards of half or more of their books at a 50 percent discount, you might request a provision stating that no more than 35 percent of the sales of your book will be calculated at the lower royalty (and settle for 40, 45, or even 50 percent, since these are reasonable rates).

When you are uncertain about what will happen *if* a particular situation arises or *if* a provision or clause is invoked—since it is not clear from the context in the contract—ask about it and get it spelled out in writing or in the contract if appropriate. This is especially important if that eventuality is a real possibility. Remember that unusual or unexpected scenarios can take place, and that the purpose of contracts is to foresee them and to solve them before disputes arise. An ounce of prevention. . . .

TACTIC #9: DON'T GET HUNG UP

Occasionally during the negotiation process you will reach a sticking point—some clause, provision, or phrasing on which your and the editor's horns are locked. *Put it aside* by suggesting, "Let's go back to that later." Getting bogged down will only frustrate you and the editor and may put a sharper edge on the discussion, imperceptibly causing both of you to toughen your positions on the remaining issues you want to negotiate. And that can only be to your disadvantage. Once you have worked out everything else, you can return to the unresolved problem, preferably after a day or two has passed, which will have given both of you time to consider compromise positions. With the tension dissipated and with the knowledge that you are only one step away from concluding a deal, both of you will be psychologically more disposed to compromise and to solve the problem.

TACTIC #10: REMAIN SELF-CONFIDENT

If you find that the negotiations don't seem to be going well, that you are being refused concessions or reasonable demands, that the compromises are all one-sided (yours!), or that one or more crucial requests are denied, you may want to pause and reconsider. If this editor and publisher want your book, the chances are that more than one other will too, and if—on the basis of the guidelines provided in the previous chapter—you surmise that you are being reasonable but the editor isn't, it is probably true that the next house will be more accommodating. Don't forget that in order to make an offer, your editor has prepared an elaborate profit-and-loss statement for your book that estimates that the book will be successful, and he or she has persuaded the marketing department as well as one or more executives (and probably others in the firm too) that your book is worth risking a capital investment in excess of $10,000. Out of scores of other worthy projects, an editor has chosen yours as one of the twelve to twenty or so books a year that he or she wants to publish. You have *something of value* to offer this or some other publisher, something in which you have—or will have—invested an inordinate amount of time and energy. Sometimes it is worthwhile to take a stand, refuse the offer, and try elsewhere.

TACTIC #11: CALL THE BLUFF

A successful negotiation requires a willingness to call the publisher's bluff; or, conversely, a willingness on your part to lose. In order to get your minimum requirements, you have to be prepared to say, "No, this is my bottom line." Unless you *approach* the negotiation with that attitude firmly fixed, you are probably in for trouble, for either party in a negotiation should be (and the editor will be) attuned to the unsaid, the subliminal, the subtle indications that communicate whether or not you *really* mean it. However, as any good card player or negotiator knows, there are several stages and degrees between the first request and the absolute minimal requirement, where "No," for example, may mean "Maybe." How to play well in this netherland is a function of talent and experience and cannot be conveyed in a paragraph or two. If you have done it in other situations, now is the time to employ what you have learned.

Bearing in mind, before you begin, that this doesn't have to be your last-ditch stand, that you have something valuable to offer that someone else will want if this house won't meet your minimum requirements, will make it easier for you to act with assurance and self-confidence, which in themselves are strong assets in any negotiation.

If you do finally say no and abort the negotiation, don't do it curtly or in anger, or just fail to return the editor's call. Do it pleasantly, recognizing that the editor is usually not the person calling the shots—executives in the firm, fixed house policy, an uncertainty about how many copies your book can sell, or any number of other possible reasons may have determined the line the editor has drawn. Moreover, you never know when you may want to come back to that editor with another book, or whether—a day or a week later—you may reconsider your position and change your mind.

In such a situation, if you return to the editor soon enough, the chances are better than 50/50 that you can resume the negotiation and make a deal. You are not losing face, and you won't be the first writer (or the first agent) to do so. Don't expect, however, a corresponding change of heart by the editor; when an editor says, "Definitely no," he or she usually means just that. Since editors are accustomed to winning some and losing some (especially when they are bidding against other houses, a common occurrence), they rarely cry over spilt milk.

TACTIC #12: LEARN TO JUGGLE

It is clear from the queries agents and editors receive that many writers make multiple submissions to both, but only half the time will writers indicate that they have done so. As a consequence, I generally add to my reply, if I am interested in pursuing the project, that I want to read the sample or completed manuscript, "provided you assure me that I am the only agent considering it for a period of three weeks." I usually get that assurance, so long as I reply quickly enough to the query, but sometimes I don't get an answer or I get a "No, thanks." It may be my own quirk that in *most* instances I don't wish to compete with other agents, or perhaps to wind up spending half a day reading a book and deciding I want to take it on, only to be told, "Thanks, but I am going with X, Y, or Z."

With editors, however, the scenario can be slightly different. To protect yourself from unpleasant consequences—and I will spare you a long-winded explanation of the possibilities—*always* indicate that you are making a multiple submission, by stating at the end of your *original* covering letter (very few editors take photocopied queries seriously) that you are "sharing this submission with several other editors." You needn't mention the number or the names. Some editors will not respond to a multiple submission from an author without an agent. But many will, if it is a good one, and even if only three out of six respond, you have still saved a lot of time.

Writers who have asked me about this generally have only one concern: "What do I do if all six editors want my book?" As my father says, "You should be so lucky." But how *do* you juggle a multiple submission? If you send only a query letter, you can submit your sample or manuscript to the first editor who responds and inform him or her that you will not submit it elsewhere if you have a decision within three or four weeks. Or you can send your materials to that editor and say, "I expect a few responses in the next week or two and I would appreciate hearing from you on or by such and such a date" (four to five weeks later). This provides imaginary competitors in the wings who you hope will materialize in the next week or two, so that you *do* have more than one interested party, and, eventually, perhaps two or more bidders. Similarly, if you skip the query stage and begin by submitting an outline and sample chapters or an entire manuscript to several houses, you should end your letter by stating, "I am sharing this with several houses and would like to hear from you on or by. . . ."

Before we go to Act Two and your fantasies run away with you, let me point out that in my experience, only those writers who have strong track records are likely to provoke a bidding war, as may those *very* few projects that are clear candidates for impressive paperback reprint or subsidiary rights sales. In most cases, when I make a multiple submission, I am happy to get one reasonable offer. If it appears to me that a book *is* in either of those categories, then I hold an "auction," a more rigorous form of a multiple submission that I do not recommend for authors without agents. If your book seems to be in that category, you are better off using an agent.

If after several weeks you do get an offer, and it is higher than your minimum requirement, you will effusively thank the editor and point out that you have one (or more) other interested houses (no names) and must honor the final date you set. The offer is usually confined to the amount of the advance against royalties, but you will also want to ask what the royalties are, whether the book is to be published in hardcover or paperback, and what potential the editor thinks the book has vis-à-vis first year's sales and subsidiary rights. You will also want to raise your few crucial points. Most editors will accept having to wait, since you are now playing by the rules. If—as rarely happens—you are pressured to make a decision or risk losing the offer, you may counter by saying that you would consider a "preemptive bid," but it would have to be much higher (say, twice the offer). A preemptive bid is one that is high enough to persuade a writer to forgo playing out the hand. It is a sum almost as high as, or higher than, one would expect from the top bidder. Guessing the appropriate numbers in this situation would be just as difficult for an agent as it would be for you.

The editor may then (or up to a day later) offer a compromise figure, which you can accept (using this leverage to improve on all the terms) or sweetly reject, saying that you feel you want to play out the hand (you are very unlikely to lose this first bidder). If in the unlikely event that you do get and accept a preemptive bid, you should immediately notify any other interested editors by phone.

After receiving your first bid, you inform the other interested parties (or their assistants) by phone that you have a firm offer for X dollars, and you hope to hear from them on or before your closing date. (If this scenario is making you nervous, now might be the time to call an agent or a lawyer for help.)

The morning of your closing date, by which time you may or may not have an offer, call all the editors who haven't responded. If you have a first offer, you generally are expected to conclude the deal that day, or the next, and usually must wistfully set adrift those editors who plead for more time, as you risk losing your offer by extending the negotiations more than one day past the closing date.

If you get a second offer (which ought to be higher than the first; I am usually not moved by explanations about how much better house A can do for my client than any other house, although it is *sometimes* true), you continue calling on this "first round" until you see whether you have yet a third or fourth or fifth offer (don't expect it!). Then, go out to lunch to collect your thoughts.

You should have made careful notes about your offers: how much of an advance, how much in royalties, what share of rights, the editor's feelings about the book and its potential, and your few crucial points. If you feel that the main difference between the offers is the advance, during the next round your goal is to see how high it will go. You return to the first bidder, saying that you will have as many rounds as it will take to get to the highest offer or one final "best offer" (easier to handle), that there are X number of houses (remember: no names until it's over), and that you would like to verify the offer: not just the advance, but the royalties on hardcover and paperback, the rights split, and the two or three other issues that you feel are most important. (You don't want to slow things down with secondary issues or small-print negotiations, which are invariably ironed out afterward.)

In a short time, you will generally play out your hand and will probably take the best offer, bearing in mind that the leverage you have from each previous bid should be used to improve your position for the next one. You may find that royalties or rights, for instance, are not equal and may decide that you will take $3000 less in advance money but have better terms. It may be that publisher A's promise to bring your book out a season sooner is more important to you than a large advance. Each writer has to decide which inducements are most important, although most of the time the size of the advance is the key issue. Take the time to sit and think about the top offers; use your calculator to see what difference there is between 15,000 paperback copies sold at a 6 percent royalty at house A versus an 8 percent royalty at house B. Sometimes there are multiple factors to weigh, sometimes not.

Be prepared to have the bidding spill over to a second day; editors usually have to get clearance to improve offers and terms, decision-makers may be out to lunch or sick, sales managers may have to be consulted, and so forth. Two days is not uncommon. Your last move may be to go to the house that has offered the best advance but not as favorable terms as another house and point out that if it could amend the terms a bit you would be inclined to accept its offer. This often results in an improvement.

It is not uncommon to have no offer at all on your closing day; for one reason or another editors have not gotten around to presenting your book at the editorial meeting, or some key decision maker is out of town. You may have received some rejections already, but at the other houses, a book under serious consideration sometimes drags past the closing day for any of a variety of reasons. Usually, the editors will apologize and ask for a day to a week more. Make it a whole week, and then call the other interested editors and explain that a few editors need more time too, and you are putting it off for a week. In this way, you stand a better chance of having more than one house bid for your book, since only one editor may be able to report in a day, whereas several others could have a decision within a week. Once it is clear that none of the editors can make an offer on your closing day, *you* can set the closing date, and the later the better . . . up to a week.

Of course, it is possible to have no offer at all, period. Agents as well as writers make multiple submissions, and sometimes nobody shows. Now's the time for a double martini. Sleep it off and start another round the next day; I have sold books after thirty or more submissions, which required four or five rounds of multiple submissions.

When you accept the final offer—and you may be asked or expected to reveal the names of the other bidders—immediately call and notify, sympathetically but not condescendingly, the other editor(s). It is customary to reveal to these editors too what the outcome was. If you fudged, if you distorted, if you raised terms or bids on your own, you risk losing the deal whether then, or weeks or even months later; "bad faith" can be grounds for canceling a contract. Trade publishing is such a small industry, and the gossip is rife enough, that sooner or later there is a good chance of being caught, and the consequences can be unpleasant. Yes, occasionally some agents do it, but at the least, their reputations and businesses are likely to suffer, as would yours. Why risk it?

To some writers, this scenario sounds exciting (frankly, I love it, as I imagine most agents do); to others, this kind of juggling would generate so much anxiety that they wouldn't dream of entering these waters. It's up to you!

5

Representation: literary agents and lawyers

At some point most writers ask themselves, "Should I try to get an agent?" Well, it all depends. Let us first consider some other questions and some customary practices of agents and lawyers. Will agents represent poets or writers of short stories or articles? In the main, ninety-nine out of one hundred agents (agents who do *not* make their living primarily from charging editing and handling "fees" in addition to commission) will not, except under the following circumstances:

- when the client primarily writes books but has an occasional article or story to place;
- when the writer consistently gets published in top magazines (those that pay well) and is relatively prolific;
- when the writer is a celebrity or is well known for one reason or another;
- when the writer of a number of published stories or articles is setting to work on a full-length work of nonfiction or fiction;
- when the agent is trying to place selections from a book prior to publication (first serial rights).

Even under these circumstances, agents are generally reluctant to submit short pieces. The magazine market for short stories has decreased in the past ten years or so, and the competition for limited space is very keen. The number of magazines that pay $2000 and upward for either fiction or nonfiction is relatively scarce, and the 10 percent to 15 percent commission on this or lesser amounts is hardly worth the time, effort, and expense. It is virtually as much work to place a story or an article as it is to place a book. As for poetry, no agent—except those who charge fees plus commission—will take on individual poems, and the few who do represent poets for book-length collections will take on only poets who have a national reputation. There are exceptions, but they are very few in number.

Is it true that many book publishing houses will not consider unsolicited queries, samples, or manuscripts from a first-book writer? Major houses such as Simon & Schuster often return submissions with a form letter stating that they do not consider unsolicited materials or those that are not submitted through an agent. Another more common rejection form letter states, "This book does not suit our list at the moment," which usually means that a book is being rejected for any of a dozen different reasons that the publisher does not have the time or inclination to explain to or debate with you.

In point of fact, these houses have assistants or entry-level personnel who do read, however briefly, part or all of a submission. "Part" might mean a couple of sentences, for as soon as a reader comes across "I have written a 'fictional novel' " or any other indication of illiteracy or inappropriateness, he or she will put the project into a "standard rejection" pile, just as agents will. But if this first reader thinks the project worthy, he or she will respond favorably, either by requesting more material or by passing it along to an acquisitions editor—that is, the editor who has the responsibility and authority to sign books on the publisher's behalf.

The problem for the writer without an agent whose book is appropriate and publishable is that these readers are processing scores of unsolicited submissions a day and are therefore just as likely to pass over a viable book as they are to fish it out. There are two pertinent tips to follow here. To begin with, avoid going to the top two dozen houses if this is a first book, for there are at least 200 (or more) major publishers that *will* read the "slush pile" more carefully. In addition, don't address a query to "editor" or "education editor," or whomever; that's a sure way to wind up with a form letter of rejection. Instead, find out the name of an editor, preferably one who is interested in your genre.

Many writers turn to agents out of frustration rather than intention after receiving form rejection letters from a dozen or more houses. Agents are generally reluctant to take on a project that has been turned down by so many publishers, whatever the reasons. I have done it a number of times, but only when I felt that the project was worthy and that the writer had either not approached the right houses or editors or had not properly presented his or her materials. Most agents will do this, but only occasionally.

Should you try to secure an agent? This is something you should decide before you solicit publishers. And you ought to feel that you have almost as good a chance of getting an offer as an agent does. Going to an agent out of choice rather than desperation is more likely to be fruitful both in securing an agent and in working harmoniously with one. The only way to get this feeling is to learn enough about book publishing so that your approach and choice of houses is as intelligent and selective as an agent's would be. Several good books explain how to do this, and it is worthwhile to consult one or more of them (see the Recommended Reading list). The more you know about publishing and contracts, the more informed your decisions will be—for agents are supposed to offer *advice* and you are to make the decisions. Also, the less likely you are to be frustrated, angry or disappointed at some juncture in the entire process. In publishing there is many a slip 'twixt cup and lip.

Let us consider for a moment the major advantages and disadvantages of working with an agent.

ADVANTAGES

- Agents know editors personally and are more likely to get a hearing (that is, more than a perfunctory reading).
- Agents know which houses and editors are buying what kinds of books.
- Agents will invariably negotiate a better deal: more money, a larger share of rights, more protection for the author, less thorns remaining in the small print to prick the unwary writer.
- Agents can make multiple submissions or conduct auctions, maneuvers that are much trickier for authors;
- An agent can act as a buffer between you and the publisher when problems arise and can often solve them without disrupting a cordial editor/author relationship.

- Agents have more "clout" to prompt a publisher to follow through on many—but not all—of his initial honeymoon promises rather than, as often happens, letting your book fall through the cracks into oblivion.

DISADVANTAGES

- Not all agents are first-rate or capable of giving a book its best shot (and this is especially true for a first book).
- It may take a lot of time and effort to secure an agent, and if and when you do succeed, you are still on first base.
- Agents will take 10 to 15 percent of your book's income as long as your book is in print.
- An agent who does not think your book is commercial or "hot" may not put in the kind of dedicated and sustained effort to place it that you would; he or she might bow out after three, five, or ten submissions (fifteen to twenty seem to me a reasonable minimum).
- Although there are approximately 650 agents in the United States, only a few of them may suit you or your book. How are you going to locate the right one?
- Agents have contacts with editors at virtually all the top houses, and at many of the smaller ones too, but they generally favor a few dozen and rarely step beyond the one hundred or so brand-name houses. Yet your book might be an ideal candidate for a smaller house that the agent has never worked with or just doesn't consider worth his or her time.

There are other advantages and disadvantages, but these lists cover most of the important points. While you weigh these pros and cons you should also think about what reception the sort of book you are writing will meet with at an agency or a publishing house.

A work of fiction, if it is "literary"—as opposed to being a genre (mystery, adventure, science fiction, romance) or "commercial" novel—is *very* hard to place. It is likely to be difficult to get the novel read at a trade house, so, although you may have a hard time securing representation for it, you are still probably better off trying to find an agent first. Commercial fiction and genre fiction are more likely to be looked at closely even if submitted "over the transom."

With nonfiction, those books that have a very specifically defined audience—such as *How to Do Your Own Wallpapering*, *A Traveler's Guide to Deserts of North America*, or *The Zucchini Cookbook*—are almost as easy for the first-book writer to place as for an agent. The same is true of books that primarily have a regional appeal, such as *Biking Trails of Western Manitoba*. The key to early success is choosing the proper publisher—that is, submitting to those houses that bring out books which complement (but don't directly compete with) your own project. They should be houses that have books in those categories or genres *on their current or forthcoming list* (the "direction" of a house sometimes changes in six months or a year). Manuscripts in other areas of nonfiction, such as self-help (*How to Have a Creative Fight with Your Spouse*), diet or exercise, current events, and parenting, have a more difficult time getting serious attention if they are unsolicited and if the author lacks a "name," expert credentials, or some demonstrable influence with the book's intended audience.

But if you submit your book to a specific editor at a suitable trade house, *and* the book is marketable (i.e., has a potential first year's sales of 6000 to 7500 in hardcover, 10,000 to 15,000 in a trade paperback format, or 25,000 and up for a mass market format), *and* your query or sample is well written and compelling, *and* you show that what you have to say hasn't already been said better, you are bound to get the kind of day in court you deserve from three to four out of five houses. This is the same as an agent's batting average.

There are types of books that, by and large, neither agents nor editors at national trade houses are likely to sign up. In these cases you may be better off submitting to a small, regional, or university press or a vanity press. Other options are to self-publish or to not write at all.

Poetry and short-story collections have an exceedingly slim chance of being published unless you have a national reputation and have been published in *many* recognized magazines and journals. Academic dissertations (unless revised, and then only if they potentially have a more than modest audience), monographs on special topics, and other scholarly books generally won't interest an agent or a national trade publisher (although there are many good professional and academic houses, not to mention university presses, that may take them).

Books on fads that have passed or are even now highlighting the best-seller lists but will be ancient history by the time they are published (as I write this, break-dancing is such an example) are also *libri non grata*. I still get proposals for books on the Rubik's Cube, running, or pocket calculators—but they are years overdue. Books on how to cure America's or the world's ills, whether economically, politically, socially, or in the classroom, fall on deaf ears unless you are as prominent as John Kenneth Galbraith, Ralph Nader, Dr. Joyce Brothers, or John Holt. Ditto for autobiographies or biographies, unless you or your subject has a name that many will recognize. Books on exercise, diet, parenting, real estate, investing, and other ways to improve people's lives or fortunes may frequently make the best-seller lists, but unless you have very impressive credentials and experience and something truly novel to say, you will probably get short shrift from agents and editors. Books about your experiences in a war, emigrating, triumphing over a severe illness or a nasty divorce, or being persecuted by the tax man (or any other bureaucrat) usually do not have an audience outside of your own circle. Let us stop here, although this list is by no means exhaustive; almost half the submissions received by me and other agents fall into one of these unlikely-to-be-published categories.

The last question we will consider about agents, but by no means the last word about them (see the Recommended Reading list for several books on agents and their practices), is whether to approach one before or after you have a nibble or a commitment from a publisher.

Some writers have the notion that the primary function of an agent is to find them a publisher, any publisher. A number seem to feel that now that they have failed on their own, it is time for an agent to take over. Others decide that, rather than go through the wearying, frustrating, and unrewarding task of making the rounds, they prefer to have someone else do the plodding.

Agents do not view their role this way. As you can see from the advantages listed earlier, finding a publisher, any publisher, is not a primary function. Finding the *right* publisher, getting the best deal, and so forth are the *raisons d'être* for agents. It is patently obvious that Saul Bellow and Gail Sheehy do not need agents to find them a publisher, and that several thousand other writers don't either. To earn a living as an agent, one has to have a roster of clients whose works are consistently publishable and who do not represent a gamble in terms of time, effort, and expense. Every book I take on represents an investment of several hundred dollars; if I don't place the book, and therefore don't make a commission, then I have effectively lost that money. It follows that *for the most part* I must be conservative in my choice of clients, for I don't get a salary or a pension and I have to pay my overhead.

Thus, like publishers, agents are cautious about taking on the first-book writer or the iffy project and are generally quite selective. On the other hand, it is still true that almost all agents are receptive to first-book writers and offbeat books, since we are all stimulated by new projects, good writing, and a challenge; moreover, it is self-evident that the next generation of classics, best-sellers, and backlist titles has to start with a first book. Also, even though taking on a first book is an investment and a gamble (some more so; some less so), the stakes aren't as substantial as they are for a publisher, where the cost of producing and launching even a modest book runs to $10,000 and upward.

You can therefore conclude that if you have already published a book with a recognized house—provided that the book has had some reasonably good reviews and sales—or have found an editor who wants to publish your first book, it should be relatively easy to find a good agent. If you have not published before and you do not have an interested publisher, it is obviously going to be a bit harder. Based on what we have discussed so far, there are not only pros and cons to weigh, but also some whens and ifs to consider. And bear in mind that, temperamentally, some writers are more suited to working with agents than others.

If you decide that you do want to work with an agent, it is always better to go to one before approaching publishers. If you strike out with six or twelve or twenty-four agents, you still have the world of book publishers open to you, whereas the reverse is not necessarily true. Moreover, you can always go back to agents once you have found a publisher, and you will generally succeed this time around.

Since this book is a guide to doing it yourself, you may have found this discussion academic and superfluous. On the other hand, you may feel that our exploration has enlightened you but put you no closer to a decision. You may find it easier to make a decision once you have talked to an agent or two. There is no reason for you not to query and talk to an agent interested in your project (few will consult with you over the phone *before* seeing an outline and sample) before making a decision. Why not test the waters if you are curious? While you are mulling this over, let us consider an option that never occurs to many writers: the lawyer as agent.

One primary distinction between using a lawyer and using an agent is that lawyers will not canvass publishers or make submissions; their services as negotiators are available only when and if you have already secured an offer or a commitment from an editor or a publisher (except, of course, for those few lawyers who operate their own agencies). However, there are instances in which a writer might employ a lawyer during or after contracting with a publisher. For example, one might ask a lawyer to review the contract before signing it—whether the writer has an agent or not—to see if there are snags or provisions that might result in a problem. When you have an agent, however, unless the book is clearly a potential legal problem (perhaps involving libel, invasion of privacy, or a copyright complication), that agent will be sufficiently familiar with the legal ramifications and therefore relatively competent to discuss, negotiate, and resolve them. Or a writer might feel, once the manuscript is delivered, in production, or even published, that the publisher has failed to provide the minimum adequate performance every writer is entitled to expect and receive—which is implicit in any publishing contract even if not explicitly stated in yours—and decide to resort to some pressure or even a suit.

But for our purposes, let us consider only the options that are relevant to contract negotiations. You have an offer from an editor, or you expect one, and you have not yet committed yourself to that offer or that house. What services can a lawyer provide, what might they cost, how do they differ from the services of an agent, and under what circumstances might you decide to choose a lawyer rather than an agent?

Like an agent, a lawyer can negotiate all aspects of a contract, including the amount of the advance, the royalties, all the small print, and the potential legal pitfalls (maybe doing a better job on these), as well as the share of rights. On this last point, however, lawyers will not—as agents do—exercise or exploit certain rights on the author's behalf.

Traditionally, agents will in many cases retain 100 percent of first serial, performance, and foreign rights (and occasionally some others) on your behalf. Furthermore, they will attempt to sell or license these rights, at the appropriate time and if a sale seems at all possible, either on their own, in conjunction with a colleague abroad, or, in the case of performance rights, with a colleague on the West Coast. A lawyer *could* also retain 100 percent of these rights on a writer's behalf, but as the lawyer does not usually have the facilities or the inclination to sell or license them—and most writers would find it difficult and complicated to do themselves—it is not customary for them to do so. Therefore, most lawyers would try to negotiate the best possible share of these rights short of 100 percent, although some literary lawyers will retain 100 percent and steer their clients to performance-rights agents or foreign-rights agents, either here or abroad (some agents handle foreign rights for some U.S. agents but work, in turn, with co-agents abroad).

When writers (or agents) retain 100 percent of any subsidiary right, it means that in exercising it—for instance, in selling a chapter to be published in a magazine before book publication—they pocket 100 percent of any money received from that sale or license as soon as a check is received. (Writers who do this should remember that, ultimately, the publicity value is more important than the first serial fee and should not concentrate solely on high-paying or glamorous media.) However, when publishers—in effect acting as the writer's agent—license or sell this right, they are entitled by contract to deduct the author's share, even if it is 90 percent of that right, from the "unearned balance"—that is, the amount of the advance against royalties that has not yet been earned by the sale of the book. Some publishers will agree to a pass-through provision of first serial, British Commonwealth, and foreign rights, within thirty to sixty days of receipt, *before* the advance is earned out.

In practical terms: If you receive a $10,000 advance, and prior to book publication your publisher sells a chapter to a magazine for $1500, your 90 percent (if that is the split; it can range from 50/50 to 90/10), which is $1350, appears on the first statement as "earned income," so that you now have an *unearned* balance of $8650 (provided the book hasn't sold a single copy). The clear disadvantages to the publisher's control of these rights are that at best you may have to wait as much as one or two years from the publication date to "see" that additional income; at the worst, your book will not sell enough copies to earn back the advance, and you may never enjoy the fruits of that rights sale.

But this drawback is merely one factor to weigh, so let us consider some others. Whereas literary lawyers will extract a handsome fee of $150 to $250 per hour for their services, it is nonetheless a one-time fee. An agent will collect 10 to 15 percent of your book's earnings as long as the book is in print or is generating income from some other source. Another important consideration is that a good agent will hold your hand, so to speak, throughout the life of the book. Problems can and usually do arise, whether during editing ("You want me to drop that entire chapter?"), production ("But you assured me I would have a four-color jacket!—this one's awful!"), publicity ("You've booked me on one radio call-in show in Tulsa and that's *it?*"), or distribution ("The Waldenbooks store in my own hometown hasn't had a single copy in stock and the book has been out a month!"). It means a lot to have an ally at any of these junctures, even if only to commiserate with you or to explain why "they" haven't taken out an ad in the *New York Times Book Review* for your book.

Lawyers generally don't involve themselves in these matters unless a legal issue is at stake, and if they do, their clock begins ticking at $100 an hour or more. Also, they are usually not as experienced or adept at wheedling, cajoling, or embarrassing your editor as agents are; lawyers' talents tend more to the art of loquacious intimidation.

But there are circumstances under which a writer might be better off employing an attorney: when large sums are involved (say, an advance of $75,000 or more and potential sub rights, such as a paperback reprint sale, for even higher stakes) or when tax complications might arise, such as an estate problem or a pending divorce.

As most of us know, there are general-practice lawyers, as well as those who specialize in such areas as tax law, estates, personal injury, and criminal law. One other field is the arts, which encompasses the entertainment media and publishing, whether of newspapers, books, or magazines, and includes the subspecialty of copyright law. An educated guess at the number of lawyers in this country with experience and special competence in book publishing contracts is about 250. These "literary lawyers" are clustered in New York City and the greater Los Angeles area, but a scattering are found in most major cities. Although it is comforting to know that your lawyer is just across town and a twenty-five-cent call away, there is little disadvantage to working with a lawyer 3000 miles away (as with agents).

The advantages of working with a literary versus a general-practice lawyer are clear: Someone familiar with the ground rules in publishing and house policy at major publishers, with a sense of what a "property" is worth, and with a sense of how far you can push, so to speak, with book publishers is likely to get a better deal in a shorter time and with less fuss. By "fuss," I mean that many general-practice lawyers may find certain standard provisions in book contracts unfair or unreasonable and may attempt to have them deleted entirely or modified more radically than most publishers would allow. And some nonspecialists will not even recognize the worst provisions. Lawyers familiar with these industry-wide conventions will attempt to improve these pernicious provisions, but within the framework of what is generally acceptable.

On the other hand, if you already have a family lawyer or prefer to work with someone locally, working with either of them may still be preferable to employing no lawyer at all, especially if you feel that you would be a weak negotiator. If your lawyer is not familiar with publishing contracts, he or she will (or should) contact a colleague with experience in this field and consult on issues that are unfamiliar. Also, the cost may be much lower. Fees for literary lawyers currently range from $150 to $250 per hour. For a book publishing contract that presents no special complications, the fee will run to approximately $500. Your own lawyer, or a local one, may charge no more than half that amount. Even if you do negotiate your own contract, it is a worthwhile investment to have a literary lawyer or your own lawyer review the contract. There are always some points that you should attend to but don't, small print to question, or matters pertinent to your particular book that a lawyer can help with, if only to explain the ramifications. If nothing else, this consultation may give you temporary peace of mind.

To locate a literary lawyer, a writer can call the local bar association (or one in the nearest large city), which can usually advise a writer and supply some names. Or one can consult the *Legal Directory*, published by Martindale-Hubbell, which contains a state-by-state list of attorneys, along with an indication of their specialties.

For those impecunious writers who do not earn a living wage—according to reliable statistics gathered only a few years ago, the median annual income for writers is the paltry sum of $4800 a year—a special opportunity exists. Volunteer Lawyers for the Arts (VLA) is an association of attorneys throughout the country, in approximately thirty separate and unrelated offices, who supply *free* legal advice for those in the arts, provided that their income qualifies them. These organizations are partly supported by grants from places such as the National Endowment for the Humanities, and many have suffered as a result of cutbacks in the past few years. Currently, for example, Los Angeles, of all places, no longer has a VLA office. Most of these thirty-odd organizations cannot afford full-time staff members (New York City, at the moment, is an exception as is San Francisco's Bay Area Lawyers for the Arts [BALA]), and employ part-time para-professionals or volunteers who answer phones and reply to mail.

VLA is available to actors, dancers, photographers, musicians, painters, and a host of other artists, not to mention writers, who make up about 10 percent of the clientele. Generally, for a modest fee of $15 to $35, an artist will be interviewed and then referred to an attorney who specializes in the kind of law needed. This attorney will provide the service free of charge—except for direct out-of-pocket expenses, such as long-distance calls or photocopying—if the writer's income is below an amount stipulated by that particular office. This sum must include the "gross household income" (or some similar formula). That is, if you earn $4800 a year writing but your spouse earns $22,500 from teaching, you may not qualify. In order to determine eligibility, a writer should contact the nearest VLA office, whose address or phone number the local bar association can provide. However, a writer need not use the closest VLA; he or she may contact any one of them throughout the country (one of which may have an income-eligibility figure you meet). Incidentally, BALA does *not* have a means test, and clients get the first half hour free.

The attorney you will be referred to is the same one who would charge $175 per hour if a writer didn't qualify for free assistance. What could be better? (Not being so poor could be much better.) The one drawback to VLA assistance is that the negotiation or problem is going to have to wait for about three to five weeks, which is the average amount of time it takes from the first contact with the VLA until an attorney can put in some time on the writer's behalf.

Agent, lawyer, do-it-yourself; these are the options. Now that you understand what is involved in negotiating contracts, it should be easier for you to make a decision. Whichever you choose, I hope that you now feel more fortified to understand the process and the documents, to realize what the stakes are, and to get yourself a better deal. Good luck!

Recommended reading

MAGAZINE AGREEMENTS

The ASJA Handbook (New York: American Society of Journalists and Authors, Inc., 1985). A forty-two-page pamphlet containing the AS-JA's code of ethics and fair practices, with chapters on selling articles and books, writing for corporations, and a recommended standard letter of agreement. Practical, up-to-date, sound guidelines for all writers; well worth the somewhat inflated $5.95 price.

Deimling, Paula (ed.), *Writer's Market* (Cincinnati: Writer's Digest Books, annual). Contains more than 1500 listings of magazines looking for fiction, nonfiction, and poetry, as well as listings of trade, technical, and professional journals, with detailed guidelines for the kinds of material wanted, length, terms, rates, policy, appropriate submission procedures, and so forth. Also contains a number of useful essays on writing and marketing for almost all categories, from plays to gags.

Fredette, Jean M. (ed.), *Fiction Writer's Market* (Cincinnati: Writer's Digest Books, annual). Contains listings for approximately 300 commercial and 500 "little" (literary and alternative/counterculture) magazines that buy fiction, as well as more than thirty articles on how to write it. Most of the listings can be found in *Writer's Market* and are sometimes more detailed and useful than those found here.

Freedman, Helen Rosengren, and Krieger, Karen, *The Writer's Guide to Magazine Markets: Non-fiction* (New York: New American Library, 1983). Explores 125 magazines in more depth than any of the annuals listed here, with guidelines on virtually all matters of importance to writers vis-à-vis these magazines. Each selection includes an interview with a (then) current acquiring editor. This book ought to be an annual, as the information is accurate, precise, thorough, and extremely useful. Worth buying even if somewhat dated.

Fulton, Len, and Ferber, Ellen (eds.), *The International Directory of Little Magazines and Small Presses.* (Paradise, California: Dustbooks, annual). Contains the most thorough listing of roughly 3000 literary/independent/alternative/counterculture magazines and book publishers looking for fiction, poetry, and nonfiction, with detailed information regarding policy, terms, rates, and so forth.

Krieger, Karen, and Freedman, Helen Rosengren, *The Writer's Guide to Magazine Markets: Fiction* (New York: New American Library, 1983). See companion volume for nonfiction (above).

Magazine Industry Market Place (New York: R. R. Bowker, annual). An annotated listing of more than 2500 magazines, of which roughly 700 are devoted to fiction and poetry. As up to date a reference as one can find, but it contains no information for writers regarding submissions, rates, and terms.

Magazines for Libraries, 4th ed. (New York, R. R. Bowker, 1982). An annotated listing of more than 6500 U.S. periodicals, culled from a total of approximately 65,000 (!). The fifth edition is due out in Fall/Winter 1986. Although the annotations are not as detailed as those for *Magazine Industry Market Place*, this volume contains almost three times as many listings. Even more complete are *Ulrich's International Periodicals* and *Ayres Periodicals Directory*, but neither is annotated.

CONTRACTS AND NEGOTIATION

Bunnin, Brad, and Beren, Peter, *Author Law and Strategies* (Berkeley: Nolo Press, 1983). The most thorough, detailed, and authoritative coverage available for writers on matters of literary law, copyrights, negotiations, magazine agreements, book publishing contracts, marketing and promotion, and so forth. Very informal and readable, and replete with examples, cases, vignettes, and sample contracts and letters. This is the one to own.

Crawford, Tad, *The Writer's Legal Guide* (New York: Hawthorn/Dutton, 1977). A practical how-to and guide on legal matters, contracts, negotiations, tax breaks, and copyright, although the advice on negotiations is not as realistic as it might be for those writers who don't write best-sellers.

Curtis, Richard, *How to Be Your Own Literary Agent* (Boston: Houghton Mifflin Company, 1984). Chatty and very readable; sensible and detailed advice on how to do it yourself from a well-known and successful agent. A real pro tells it like it is, with some sober and eye-opening criticisms of publishing practices.

LITERARY AGENTS

Cleaver, Diane, *The Literary Agent and the Writer* (Boston: The Writer, Inc., 1984). One of only two books available devoted solely to agents, covering such topics as: do you need one? how to submit, how they work, what they can do for new writers, author/agent relations, and agreements.

Larsen, Michael, *A Working Marriage: What Writers Should Know About Literary Agents* (Cincinnati: Writer's Digest Books, 1986). As the title says, this brief book explores the world of the agent and his relations with both writers and editors. Of particular use is the practical and realistic information on what agents can and can't do and what to expect, as well as the advice on finding, choosing, and keeping an agent.

Literary Agents of North America (New York: Author Aid/Research Associates International, annual). An enormously useful reference for writers looking for agents—of which about 650 are listed—since there are five indexes, including geographical and subject, so that writers can easily determine which agents are interested in a particular genre, among other things. It contains a useful introductory essay for new writers with tips on how, what, and where to submit.

MISCELLANEOUS

Appelbaum, Judith, and Evans, Nancy, *How to Get Happily Published*, 2nd rev. ed. (New York: New American Library, 1982). Chatty and optimistic but generally down-to-earth and supportive advice geared to novice writers on the how, what, and where of breaking into print, with an elaborate and useful resource section of books, people, places, and programs.

Balkin, Richard, *A Writer's Guide to Book Publishing*, 2nd rev. ed. (New York: Hawthorn/Dutton, 1981). A detailed and realistic overview of how book publishing works, from proposal submission to marketing, with additional chapters on decision making in publishing, negotiations, manuscript preparation, and book production.

Gross, Gerald, *Editors on Editing*, 2nd rev. ed. (New York: Harper & Row, Publishers, Inc., 1985). Twenty-four very readable essays by working editors in all genres and categories of book publishing on what they do and how they do it. Writers will find this insider's view a thorough and enjoyable exploration of how their most important link in the publishing process operates.

Norwick, Kenneth P., and Chasen, Jerry Simon, with Kaufman, Henry R., *The Rights of Authors and Artists* (New York: Bantam Books, 1984). An American Civil Liberties Union handbook and guide to legal rights and issues for writers and artists, by two very knowledgeable attorneys, covering copyrights, contracts, libel and privacy, obscenity, and business and tax matters. A brief reference work but well worth having on the shelf.

Polking, Kirk, *Law and the Writer*, 3rd rev. ed. (Cincinnati: Writer's Digest Books, 1985). How to understand, avoid, or cope with writers' legal problems, with new chapters (to this edition) on advertising, entertainment, and broadcasting law, as well as writers' estates. Among other matters, advice on libel, sub rights, photography, and even retirement planning. A thorough, well-rounded, and very useful reference and handbook for any writer; well worth owning.

The Writing Business (New York; Poets and Writers, Inc., 1985). A collection of more than forty articles culled from the past ten years of *Coda* magazine, by staff writers and freelancers, on all aspects of the business side of publishing, from a writer's will to a description of twenty-one writers' colonies. The wide range of unusual topics—the second novel, the poet as businessperson, starting your own small press, writing pornography—and the very informed and often elegant writing make this instructive and delightful volume well worth the $11.95 purchase price

Index

7-10; assertiveness in, 11; leverage in, 8, 19; reference books in, 9; starting point for, 10
New Grub Street, 88
Novelty books, 92

Original characters, licensing from juvenile books, 94
Orwell, George, essays, 4

Pamphlets, small press, 104
Paperback books: children's, 92; mass market, 44, 91; teenage romance, 92; trade, 44-46, 55-57, 89, 90, 91
"Pass-through" clause, 60-62, 92, 135
Performance rights, 4, 58-59, 79, 135
Permissions budget, 30-31, 97
Photocopying permission, 59
Photographs, 14-15, 79
Plagiarism, 68-69
Poetry, 10, 13, 18-19, 131; agent for, 127, 128
Pricing, book, 39
Professional and reference books, 87, 100-02; advance, 101; defined, 100; royalties, 101-02; subsidiary rights, 102
Profit consideration of editors and publishers, 3
Proofs, book, 36, 37
Provisions, contract, defined, 21
Publicity, book, 52, 53, 135

Query, book, 128
Query letter, magazine, 12, 14

Rack jobber, 89
Radio rights. *See* Performance rights
Rates, magazine, 8, 9, 10, 11
"Readers," college textbook, 97
Reader's Digest, 8, 16
Reference books. *See* Professional and reference books
Regional books, 87, 103, 131
Rejection of book manuscript, 34, 128
Religious books, 87
Remainder sales, book, 45-46
Representation by literary agents and lawyers, 127-38; *See also* Agent, literary; lawyers; first

book writer, 130-33; vs self, 129, 131; types of books for, 130-32
Reprints, hardcover book, 90
Returns, book, 63, 90, 96
Revised edition of book, 72, 73-74, 98, 100
Riders to book contract, 21, 84-85
Rights. *See also* Subsidiary rights, trade book; Contract, trade book; book club, 50, 53-54, 102; and foreign co-agent, 27-28; magazine, 10, 15-17, 19; negotiating, 10, 115; small press book, 105; and sub-agent, 27; textbook, 97-98; trade book, 24, 27-28, 127-28; university press book, 104
Romance novel book packager, 94
Royalties, book, 24; from book club sale, 54, 55; and book packager, 94; children's, 93, 94; illustrated, 93; juvenile, 93, 95; library edition, 93; mass market, 91-92; professional and reference, 101-02; small press, 105; specialized, 87-88; text-, 88, 95-97, 98, 99-100; trade book, 28, 31-32, 35, 37, 42-46, 61-65, 73-74; university press, 103-04; young adult, 93
Royalty statement, 61-65, 76

Sales, book, 28, 43-46, 88, 92, 103, 105
Scholarly books, 131
Scientific books. *See* Professional and reference books
Series books, 92, 94-95
Short story, 7, 8, 18-19, 127-28, 131
"slush pile," 128
Small press books, 87-89, 104-06; advance, 105; model contract for, 106; royalties, 105
Specialized books, 87-89
Spin-offs, children's book, 94, 95
Stage rights. *See* Performance rights
Subsidiary rights, trade book, 24, 28, 51-61, 87, 135; book club, 54-55; Braille, large print, 59; British Commonwealth, 55; commercial and merchandising, 58; electronic, 58-59; first serial, 52-53; foreign language, 55; hardcover reprint, 57; newspaper serialization, 53; paperback reprint,

About the Author

RICHARD BALKIN has had his own literary agency in New York City for more than thirteen years. Through it he represents more than fifty writers. His previous publishing experience includes working as a book sales representative, as an editor, and then as executive editor for Bobbs-Merrill, a major trade and textbook publisher. He is a former agent and publishing consultant for the Ford Foundation and a charter contributing editor to *American Poetry Review*, has taught courses in book publishing at Herbert Lehman College in New York City and at the University of Massachusetts, has lectured at writers' conferences, and has written articles for *McCall's*, *Working Woman*, *Writer's Digest*, *Coda*, *After Dark*, and *Modern Maturity*. His book *A Writer's Guide to Book Publishing* (Hawthorn/Dutton, 1977; 2nd revised ed., 1981) has sold more than 40,000 copies in hardcover and paperback editions.

Other Books of Interest

General Writing Books
Beginning Writer's Answer Book, edited by Polking and Bloss $14.95
Getting the Words Right: How to Revise, Edit and Rewrite, by Theodore A. Rees Cheney $13.95
How to Get Started in Writing, by Peggy Teeters $10.95
How to Write a Book Proposal, by Michael Larsen $9.95
How to Write While You Sleep, by Elizabeth Ross $12.95
Law & the Writer, edited by Polking & Meranus (paper) $10.95
Knowing Where to Look: The Ultimate Guide to Research, by Lois Horowitz $16.95
The 29 Most Common Writing Mistakes & How to Avoid Them, by Judy Delton $9.95
Writer's Encyclopedia, edited by Kirk Polking $19.95
Writer's Market, edited by Paula Deimling $19.95
Writer's Resource Guide, edited by Bernadine Clark $16.95
Magazine/News Writing
Complete Guide to Writing Nonfiction, by The American Society of Journalists & Authors $24.95
How to Write & Sell the 8 Easiest Article Types, by Helene Schellenberg Barnhart $14.95
Fiction Writing
Creating Short Fiction, by Damon Knight (paper) $8.95
Fiction Writer's Market, edited by Jean Fredette $17.95
Handbook of Short Story Writing, by Dickson and Smythe (paper) $7.95
How to Write Short Stories that Sell, by Louise Boggess (paper) $7.95
Storycrafting, by Paul Darcy Boles $14.95
Writing Romance Fiction—For Love and Money, by Helene Schellenberg Barnhart $14.95
Writing the Novel: From Plot to Print, by Lawrence Block $8.95
Special Interest Writing Books
The Children's Picture Book: How to Write It, How to Sell It, by Ellen E. M. Roberts $17.95
The Craft of Comedy Writing, by Sol Saks $14.95
The Craft of Lyric Writing, by Sheila Davis $17.95
How to Make Money Writing Fillers, by Connie Emerson (paper) $8.95
How to Write a Cookbook and Get It Published, by Sara Pitzer, $15.95
How to Write a Play, by Raymond Hull $13.95
How to Write & Sell (Your Sense of) Humor, by Gene Perret $12.95
How to Write the Story of Your Life, by Frank P. Thomas $12.95
Mystery Writer's Handbook, by The Mystery Writers of America (paper) $8.95
TV Scriptwriter's Handbook, by Alfred Brenner (paper) $9.95
Writing for Children & Teenagers, by Lee Wyndham (paper) $9.95
Writing After 50, by Leonard L. Knott $12.95
Writing and Selling Science Fiction, by Science Fiction Writers of America (paper) $7.95
Writing for the Soaps, by Jean Rouverol $14.95
The Writing Business
Complete Guide to Self-Publishing, by Tom & Marilyn Ross $19.95
Complete Handbook for Freelance Writers, by Kay Cassill $14.95
Editing for Print, by Geoffrey Rogers $14.95
Freelance Jobs for Writers, edited by Kirk Polking (paper) $7.95
How to Get Your Book Published, by Herbert W. Bell $15.95
How to Understand and Negotiate a Book Contract or Magazine Agreement, by Richard Balkin $11.95

To order directly from the publisher, include $2.00 postage and handling for 1 book and 50¢ for each additional book. Allow 30 days for delivery.
Writer's Digest Books, Dept. B, 9933 Alliance Rd., Cincinnati OH 45242
Prices subject to change without notice.